GOD'S BIBLICAL
BLUEPRINT FOR
STRENGTHENING
YOUR MARRIAGE

Discover Biblical Strategies from Scripture to Deepen Your Bond,
Overcome Challenges, and Grow Spiritually Together

B. Mitchell-Dos Santos
&
Phelipe Dos Santos

Contents

Introduction

It wasn't the first time we had silence at home, but somehow, the quietness carried more than just the weight of unsaid words, unmet expectations, and the slow drift that happens when two hearts lose their way.

We might have been living under the same roof, sharing the same meals, managing the same mundane chores, but something had changed, and it had become undeniable.

It wasn't about the constant disagreements or how hard it was to balance life at work with family life. It was a crippling sense that, somehow, along the journey, we had begun to stop seeing one another as we once had.

I remember sitting across from my spouse one evening, feeling that void between us, and wondering how we'd gotten to this place. More importantly, how exactly did we reach this point?

It was then that I reached for the Bible in quiet desperation. I wasn't looking for an easy escape or some happy ending that only existed in fairy tales; I was looking for a helping hand, something more profound than the philosophical advice I had heard enough of by now.

And there, on those pages of scripture, I found the answer to what I never knew I was looking for. *"Submit to one another out of reverence for Christ"* (Ephesians 5:21). Submission. It was not

7

exactly a word that I had necessarily thought about much. Certainly not in the context of marriage. But sitting there with the weight of that verse on my heart, I began seeing things in a new light.

Submission, as defined by the Bible, is not relinquishing one's voice and losing one's identity; it's much more than that—choosing to put your spouse first, to love them the way Christ loves, and to serve as He serves the church. The submission I'm discussing here is rooted in humility, grace, and sacrifice.

And just like that, the course of our lives changed. It was not a magical solution that fixed every problem overnight, but it gave us a foundation from which to proceed, one rooted not in our desires nor expectations but in God's design for marriage.

From that moment forward, healing began. We slowly started practicing biblical principles of headship, submission, mutual respect, and service to reconnect with each other once again. That's where the magic began.

Over time, wounds of pride, resentment, and hurt began to fall. We learned new ways of communication that create understanding rather than conflict. We rediscovered the joy of serving one another, not out of obligation but out of love.

Most importantly, we opened our marriage to God, allowing His word to guide our paths and heal our hearts.

This personal transformation was the foundation for this book. I wrote it to share these lessons and provide a practical, scripture-based roadmap for couples who want to build a Christ-centered marriage that can withstand the challenges of modern life.

This is not another book on marriage advice but rather a helping hand grounded in the wisdom of the Bible, designed to help you apply God's truths to the realities you face every day.

God designed marriage to be a covenant, a holy bond shared by husband and wife, reflecting His relationship to the church. It's not about happiness or the fulfillment of personal desires; it's about living out God's plan, which enables the husband and the wife to get closer to each other while walking toward Him.

In a time when most people perceive marriage as disposable, God leads us to a more significant destination. A godly marriage is based on headship, submission, and mutual service—principles that are as essential today as when they were first presented in the Bible.

One may start discussing "Submission" and "Headship" and how the world often misrepresents these words. Society usually views submission as a weakness, as if one partner is resigning to the will of another.

However, the Bible has a very different perspective on the subject. As God calls us to practice it in marriage, submission is never domination or inequality. It's about sacrificial love.

The message of Ephesians 5 says husbands are called to love their wives "as Christ loved the church and gave himself up for her." That is a profound, humbling call to love selflessly and generously and to be willing to serve.

On the other hand, wives are called upon to submit to their husbands out of reverence for God, not out of fear or obligation (New International Version, 2011). Thus, mutual respect and service must be found in the marital balance of partners thriving together.

Marriage becomes a partnership when every partner strives to lift each other and live in harmony while embracing these roles of relationships. That is why a godly marriage is distinct: it will show the love of Christ and the grace of God in each relationship.

Amidst the promoted individualism and self-interest worldwide, this biblical approach to marriage offers hope for building stronger, healthier, and more fulfilling relationships.

But how do we put these principles into practice in the face of today's complexities? How can we maintain a Christ-centered marriage when life pulls people in many directions?

Dual-career pressures, social media distractions, and the complicated nature of blended families can lead to challenges for couples in ways that previous generations could not even imagine. Yet, the principles for a successful marriage have not changed.

For instance, take the problem of communication. I have known many couples who have remarked that communication is their greatest challenge, which was for me at one point. They love each other profoundly but do not find it easy to express their feelings, frustrations, and needs in a way that creates understanding rather than conflict.

But the Bible reflects profoundly on communicating with one another, especially within marriage. In James 1:19, we are challenged to be *"quick to listen, slow to speak, and slow to become angry."* What a simple but powerful principle to change how you and your spouse relate to each other.

We unintentionally rushed to prepare our defense before listening. We can quickly explain and defend ourselves, justify our actions, and point out the other person's faults.

However, we create space for intimacy when we are willing to listen from a place of empathy to hear what our spouse says and not think of striking back with objections as they speak.

Communication allows your spouse to be heard and valued, not simply insisting on what you need. In this book, we will walk through practical ways to build communication in your marriage rooted in biblical wisdom so that you can navigate even the most difficult conversations with humility and patience.

Another area many couples struggle with is staying emotionally and physically close amid a busy life. Whether the pressures are work-related, children's needs, or even life distractions, it's easy for husbands and wives to lose their connection.

God designed marriage for deep, intimate bonding that goes far beyond physical affection and aims at connecting our souls.

Genesis 2:24 says, *"that a man leaves his father and mother and is united to his wife, and they become one flesh."* This encompasses all aspects of our relationship, from the spiritual to the emotional to the physical.

As we progress in this book, we'll look for practical ways to build and maintain intimacy in your marriage. We will touch on the importance of scheduling time for each other and intentionally nurturing your emotional and spiritual intimacy through prayer, worship, and shared devotions.

Intimacy in marriage is not only limited to physical proximity but also includes vulnerability, trust, and a deep sense of connection that develops from trying to understand and being understood by your spouse.

Of course, one of the most significant causes of tension in most marriages is financial pressure. Fear and insecurity, sparked by the lack of it, have also led to verbal exchanges and resentment.

Yet again, God's Word provides counsel on how best to manage finances to bring honor to Him and peace in our relationships. Proverbs 21:5 reminds us that *"the plans of the diligent lead to profit as surely as haste leads to poverty."*

Financial management in a marriage is not limited to budgeting; it's centered on comprehending and deciding your financial goals in alignment with God's will for your family. I will outline practical steps to manage your finances with wisdom and diligence so that you and your spouse can find unity and peace over financial matters. Whether you're struggling with debt, seeking to save for the future, or just deciding on day-to-day financial decisions that every family must face, these biblical principles will help you find your way and gain confidence in your financial life.

Of course, there's the ever-present challenge of social media. We are constantly bombarded by images of seemingly perfect relationships and ideal lives on these digital media streams. It's pretty easy to fall into a comparison trap, perceiving our marriage as insufficient. We cannot measure up to the curated images on our screens, but God calls us to something higher. He calls us to authenticity, to build marriages that reflect His love and grace, not the filtered images we see online.

Real marriage is not a place of such perfection; it's the process of learning how to grow together with joys and challenges. Authenticity in marriage is about embracing the messy, chaotic, imperfect, and complex parts and the beautiful moments and understanding that God calls us to love and serve each other even when life isn't perfect.

I hope the practical ideas presented here and the knowledge that God is walking with you through each step of your marriage journey encourage you. He has a plan for you and your spouse rooted in His love and wisdom. Your marriage can thrive or struggle, but one factor remains the same: There's room for growth, healing, and deeper connection when you invite God to take the center.

I want you to open your heart to the ideas and biblical practices suggested in this book that align with the principles of God to be applied in your marriage. Be open. Transformation does not happen overnight; through faith, commitment, and perseverance, you will see the fruits of a marriage that reflects God's design- one filled with love, respect, intimacy, and joy.

Regardless of where you are in your marriage today, be assured of hope. God has a plan for your marriage - strength, renewal, and abiding love.

Let's take that first step toward a more substantial, Christ-centered marriage that can stand the test of time and reflect God's glory. As you go through this book, remember the goal is to improve your marriage. With that in mind, here are some things I want you to think about as you proceed:

1. We all have weaknesses that we need to improve on. Do not focus on what your spouse may be doing wrong; instead, remind yourself of your failures and struggles and work on those. As your relationship with the Lord grows, your marriage will improve.

2. Ask yourself how you can encourage your spouse to fulfill the role God has given them. Can you do anything to make your marriage easier or more fulfilling?

3. When you become frustrated or angry with your spouse, pray to God. Lay your hurt and anger before Him and pray that He will help your spouse grow in the areas that upset you. Pray also for patience and for God to help you forgive.

Allow this book to guide you in uncovering secrets for a godly marriage, and let yourself embrace the peace and fulfillment of living out God's truths in your relationship.

CHAPTER 1

Characteristics and Values of a Husband and Wife

Phelipe recalls a time from a few years into our marriage after our first son, Avery, was born. There was a time when I thought things were going pretty well from my perspective or from what I had been taught. I was doing my job and providing for the family. One would think I had everything together, but it didn't feel right despite all the pieces falling into place.

Brenee and I were doing all the "right" things, yet somehow, we seemed to have forgotten the reasons why we did them in the first place. After another polite conversation and quiet detachment that evening, I reached my peak frustration, not at my wife but at myself.

What was I doing wrong?

How could I succeed in just about everything else in my life yet feel that I was failing at the most critical aspect of my life: my marriage?

Like I usually do when going through an uncertain phase, I turned to prayer and asked Him to show me what I was missing. In my heart, He reminded me of what was needed for marriage. He reminded me that loving and having grace was routine and connected much more closely with Christ.

"Husbands, love your wives, just as Christ loved the church and gave himself up for her."
— (Ephesians 5:25, NIV)

At that moment, Ephesians 5:25 began echoing in my head. I knew my love had derailed into routine—it was efficient but not sacrificial. Christ loves the church with patience, perseverance, and grace, and I needed to reflect on those elements of his love in my marriage.

The first reflection I witnessed was on the concept of submission. In Ephesians 5:22, He says, *"Wives, submit to your own husbands as to the Lord."* Submission here isn't a surrender or the loss of identity but trust, respect, and mutual honor, just as Christ modeled for us. Marriage can be centered on Jesus based on mutual submission and love.

In this chapter, we will explore the biblical characteristics of husbands and wives and what it means to lead, love, and submit in ways that honor God and build up your marriage. You will find that these roles are not about commanding control or power but extend to service, humility, and sacrifice, as Christ demonstrated through His relationship with the church.

What is True Masculinity? The Characteristics and Values of a Husband

Husbands, in the same way, be considerate as you live with your wives, and treat them with respect as the weaker partner and as heirs with you of the gracious gift of life so that nothing will hinder your prayers.

— (1 Peter 3:7, NIV)

Here, Peter gives a foundational view of what true manhood is in the context of marriage. True manhood in scripture, by no stretch, has anything to do with power or control; it has to do with responsibility, respect, and understanding.

1 Peter 3:7 calls for husbands to live with their wives in a considerate and understanding manner. It's the effort to fulfill and care for one's wife's physical, emotional, and spiritual nourishment. Peter teaches that husbands should honor their wives as the "weaker partner." This does not suggest weakness or inferiority; it only implies that the husband has a physical advantage.

Husbands are called to use this strength to care for, protect, and encourage their wives, not to dominate or belittle them. Peter reminds husbands that their wives are co-heirs with them of the "gracious gift of life." This refers to the shared inheritance of eternal life in Christ, which stresses the equality and dignity of both husband and wife in God's eyes. Peter warns that a husband's failure to honor his wife can even prevent his prayers from being heard.

This emphasizes the significance of the husband-wife relationship. When a husband does not treat his wife right and does not try to understand her, it impacts not only their marriage but their spiritual path with God.

The biblical mandate of 1 Peter 3:7 calls us to deliberately live a life that involves considering and honoring one's wife. This perspective can be challenging as it is not merely an obligation but a call to execute it with love, sympathy, and sincerity.

Let's look at a few practical ways to live out 1 Peter 3:7:

- **Practice Active Listening**: Do not merely hear your wife's words, but listen to her. Sometimes, you must ask her questions, validate her feelings, and clarify that she has been heard.

- **Spend Quality Time**: Amid a busy life, make intentional time for your wife, whether through date nights, quality conversation, or activities that strengthen your marriage.

- **Serve your wife daily**: Try to find opportunities in your daily life to serve her without expecting anything in return. These could even be simple chores like cleaning the house or being an emotional support system for your wife.

These simple steps reflect the deep understanding and consideration that 1 Peter 3:7 calls for. Authentic manhood implies being there for your wife consistently and sacrificially, just like the love of Christ.

For many years, I thought I knew my place as a husband: work hard to take care of my financial needs, which was my responsibility. But as I began to study 1 Peter 3:7, God showed me that providing for my wife was much more than just "putting food on the table."

My responsibilities are also understanding her emotions, fears, and desires and honoring her in light of that understanding.

I remember one incredibly crazy season of life when we were deep into work and family responsibilities. One evening, when she was tired from a long day, I stopped her for a minute and asked her, *"How are you doing?"*

I slowed down to listen for the first time in an awfully long time. What transpired next was a conversation that opened my eyes to how I had failed to honor her emotionally. This was a defining moment in our relationship; I promised to be more intentional in understanding her and honoring her in the same way God has intended for husbands to do.

The Call to Love Sacrificially

Christ has called husbands to love their wives as Christ loves the church—sacrificially (Ephesians 5:25). "And that the goal of their sacrificial love is the promotion of their wife's well-being, especially her spiritual well-being" (Sypert, 2018). These choices can be to get up early to pray for your wife, to choose patience when frustration persists, and to put her needs before your own. This kind of love reflects Christ's heart, a love that seeks to uplift and encourage, helping your wife grow emotionally and spiritually.

True sacrificial love comes from your small choices: listening when it's easier to speak, serving without expecting anything in return, and being present even when life gets busy. When I began to focus on these small acts of love, I noticed a shift in our marriage—a more profound connection built on mutual trust and respect.

Gentle Leadership: Choosing Kindness Over Harshness

> *"Husbands, love your wives, and do not be harsh with them"*
> — Colossians 3:19

Leading in marriage is not about ruling and dominating; it refers to gentleness. Harsh words create distance; gentle words create trust. When frustration takes over, leading with kindness creates a space where love and respect will grow.

There was a time when I let stress rule my words, bringing tension to the marriage. But as I looked at Colossians 3:19, I realized the power of grace in those moments. Leading with kindness, even when it's not easy, transformed the way we communicate.

A Husband Above Reproach

Being above reproach speaks to a person who leads with integrity and faithfulness in every area. It does not mean that one is perfect, but one strives to model the character of Christ through all he does. This consistency builds trust, not only with your wife but with everybody around you.

> *"Now the overseer is to be above reproach, faithful to his wife, temperate, self-controlled."*
> — 1 Timothy 3:2

Early in my marriage, I learned that being above reproach meant showing up and being reliable, faithful, and true to my word. Integrity is not formed in significant moments but during routine choices.

Standing Firm in Faith: Leading with Courage

A strong marriage requires a foundation of faith. Paul reminds husbands to lead their families confidently and trust God when He calls them to stand firm. Therefore, standing firm in faith could be through praying or receiving spiritual direction; it is about allowing God to be at the center of your marriage and leading through the strength obtained from Him.

"Be on your guard; stand firm in the faith; be courageous; be strong."
— 1 Corinthians 16:13

It is not bold in action, but it is always the daily choice to be hopeful and prayerful in faith, even in uncertain times. Praying with my wife helped deepen our bond and strengthen our trust in God's plan for us.

What is True Femininity? The Characteristics and Values of a Wife

I remember watching my grandmother, always with grace, balance the household responsibilities yet still nurture each of her children with the wisdom, care, and attention they needed. I never saw her look rushed, yet at times, her days were so packed from morning till night. Her secret? She never lost sight of her deep faith in God. I believe she was the epitome of what I would later learn in my life to be the heart of Proverbs 31:10-31, a woman of strength, wisdom, and dignity, firmly anchored in her relationship with God. A woman is called to be strong, wise, and anchored to Christ. Only with the Lord's strength are all things possible, including fulfilling our roles as wives.

The expectations from wives can feel endless. Navigating family life, work commitments, and personal growth is no easy task. It can sometimes feel overwhelming, but I meditate over this verse when I feel like this.

"And whatever you do, in word or deed, do everything in the name of the Lord Jesus, giving thanks to God the Father through him."

— Colossians 3:17

This verse allows me to center myself and remember that no matter what I am doing, I am doing it all for the glory of God, and I should give thanks to Him daily for my very life.

The Bible does paint a beautiful picture of true femininity in Proverbs 31:10-31, one who is strong, capable, and deeply rooted in faith. They are also a helpmate for her husband to take on that supporting role.

"She is clothed with strength and dignity and laughs at the days to come."

— Proverbs 31:25

In Proverbs 31:10-31, we find a rich description of the woman exemplifying godly femininity: noble, diligent, wise, and kind. She works with her hands, takes care of her household, and is respected by her family and community.

More than that, her relationship with God defines her; she fears the Lord, drawing strength and dignity from this. True femininity is not weak; far from it. Proverbs 31 shows a working and industrious woman controlling her home and, sometimes, business. Yet, her strength is not purely in her actions but in her quiet trust in God.

She "laughs at the days to come" because life is difficult, but she knows who holds her future.

Balancing the Roles of Wife, Mother, and Professional

A woman today must balance many roles: wife, mother, employee, and leader. Proverbs 31 exemplifies how to be excellent at everything with Christ at the center of it all. It is achieved through embracing the wisdom, diligence, and kindness born out of a relationship with God.

"Wives, in the same way, submit yourselves to your own husbands so that, if any of them do not believe the word, they may be won over without words by the behavior of their wives when they see the purity and reverence of your lives"

— 1 Peter 3:1-2

Peter encourages wives to live in such a way that their behavior can speak more powerfully than words. Inner beauty—gentleness, patience, and kindness—makes a woman truly radiant. This beauty doesn't fade with time but grows more potent as it is nurtured through a Christ-centered life.

I had one friend whose marriage, because they had grown apart emotionally, wasn't working for them. The wife felt unseen, and as she began losing that sense of joy, she said during one of those moments." Healing, for me, did not come in words, but it came in prayer and trusting God to restore that relationship." 1 Peter 3 says, *"Your beauty should not come from outward adornments, such as elaborate hairstyles and the wearing of gold or fine clothes. Rather, it should be that of your inner self, the unfading beauty of a gentle and quiet spirit, which is of great worth in God's sight."* Her patience and faith reflected the inner beauty Peter speaks of, a beauty that transformed not only her heart but his as well.

"Likewise, teach the older women to be reverent in the way they live... to teach what is good. Then they can urge the younger women to love their husbands and children, to be self-controlled and pure."

— (Titus 2:3-5)

24

In Titus 2, Paul emphasizes that older women teach and mentor younger women about faith-based lifestyles. They are mainly responsible when a woman enters marriage and family life. Mentoring is critical in developing godly marriages because it gives young wives insight from those who have walked the roads they are about to travel. A call to mentor is a divine connection between generations, leading to guidance and strength for those navigating the challenges of marriage for the first time. Without a doubt, this is not only a biblical principle but a lifeline for many women.

Marriage is a journey in many ways that requires commitment, trust, and faith in God. Unique characteristics define husbands and wives, though they are meant to complement each other while forming a binding partnership, like a relationship representing Christ's love.

Therefore, a godly wife is wise, gentle, loving, strong in beauty within, and respectful. A godly husband is a responsible, caring, kind, and respectful leader. These qualities bring about marriages that honor God with blessings for the home. Of course, there is hope in the light of God that leads to renewal, growth, and deeper connections.

The couple's commitment to their roles depicts Christ's love, which would strengthen marriage through the virtues of humility, understanding, and God's guidance. This union and home are based on intentional acts of love and shared faith, which are grounds spiritually harmonious with divine purpose.

CHAPTER 2

Understanding and
Embracing Biblical Roles

Husbands and wives each have different but complementary roles within a marriage. There is equality in our God-given roles. Before creating us male and female, "God said, Let us make man in our image, after our likeness and let them have dominion" (Genesis 1:26). "Man" in this verse refers to "mankind" as a whole. Yet, in this equality, there is a distinctiveness. Genesis 2:20 refers to Adam not having a "suitable helper. Thus, females were created to be their help mate and offer companionship. As Beyers put it, "Females are equal to males in value and have a distinct role that men cannot fulfill. This does not mean one gender is more "complete" than the other or that married individuals are more "complete" than singles. Our sufficiency and completeness are in Christ alone. These truths reveal males and females are of equal value in God's eyes, and each gender reveals unique characteristics or attributes of God's image" (Beyer, 2018). Let us look at some of the different roles of husband and wife.

Leading with Love: The Husband's Role

As a husband, you can sometimes feel overwhelmed by leading your wife. Perhaps you are struggling to strike a balance between leadership and love. You desire to lead but aren't quite sure how that leadership reflects Christ's example.

Christ's leadership gives us the perfect model. *"Husbands are to love their wives as Christ loved the church—to give up his life for her"* (Ephesians 5:25, NIV).

This kind of leadership is not rooted in dominance because Christ did not lead that way. He led by sacrifice, humility, and love. He gave His life for the church, not to gain something from it but for those He loved. Likewise, husbands should lead their wives not by exercising authority over them but by leading through serving, loving, and protecting their wives. It is all about putting down his needs to become a caregiver and a nurturer of his family rather than a boss.

True headship is meek and full of love and selflessness, just as Christ demonstrated in His words,

"For even the Son of Man came not to be served but to serve."

— (Matt. 20:28)

Emotional Leadership: Reflected Through the Compassion of Christ

Emotional leadership is an essential aspect of a husband's life. Being emotionally available, present, and empathetic is as important as providing for your family. It is about listening, understanding, and connecting on another level.

"Similarly, husbands ought to love their wives as their own bodies. He who loves his wife loves himself. After all, no one ever hated their own body, but they feed and care for their body, just as Christ does the church."

— Ephesians 5:28-29

Husbands are called to nourish and provide for their wives lovingly, not just through food or deeds but also through the Word.

Spiritual Leadership: Bringing Your Family Closer to God

As spiritual leaders, husbands must lead their families toward God. Ephesians 6:4 calls for fathers to bring up their children in the training and instruction of the Lord, and Joshua 24:15 emphasizes the importance of choosing to serve the Lord together as a family.

Spiritual leadership is not as complicated as we make it look. It can be being a godly example through personal devotion or reading scripture together. My husband sets time aside to pray and spend time with the Lord. After watching him, I made sure to set aside time with the Lord daily. We started praying together, and over time, our whole family became more unified in our faith. It was not about big gestures but creating a constant, Christ-centered atmosphere in our home.

Defend the Sacred Covenant

You likely get sucked into work, societal expectations, or even the distractions of life. But as a husband, you're called to defend the sacred marriage covenant. It's not limited to providing; one needs to be vigilant and guard the relationship that God has put in your hands and make sure nothing comes between you and your wife.

"Be on your guard; stand firm in the faith; be courageous; be strong."

— 1 Corinthians 16:13

A good marriage cannot only thrive on love but also requires intentional effort. It involves prioritizing time with your partner when everything around you gets hectic, knowing that external pressures should not keep you from standing firm in love. As you take this role seriously, you become a reflection of God's unwavering commitment to His people.

Remember that defending your marriage is an act of love. In Ephesians 6:4, the husband is encouraged to lead his family spiritually. Part of that leadership involves standing firm against anything threatening to weaken the bond. Husbands, think about how you embody each of these roles. Write down a list of things you do for each of the roles mentioned above. How can you make conscious decisions to take on even more of the husband role?

Supporting with Strength: The Wife's Role

Supporting in marriage is not a sign of weakness but of strength. In Genesis 2:18, God created woman as a helper suited for man, showing that wives are meant to be strong, active partners. This means standing by your husband, sharing responsibilities, and working together to build a thriving family. Marriage is a team effort, and true support strengthens both partners. In my marriage, I stand beside my husband and strive to give him valuable wisdom, guidance, and encouragement, irrespective of what happens in life. God's design for marriage is that two people work together to glorify Him through their relationship.

Women are also called to bring wisdom and care into their marriages and contribute towards the family's good. Proverbs 31:26-27 says, *"She speaks with wisdom, and faithful instruction is on her tongue. She watches over the affairs of her household."* This is not just about managing the household but an environment of love, grace, and wisdom.

Wives play a significant role in caring for the family's spiritual well-being. Titus 2:4-5 advises older women to teach younger women to love their husbands and their children, to be self-controlled, pure, and kind, and that they may also be fruitful in Christ. In doing so, wives create a Christ-honoring atmosphere in which faith grows and is handed down. Wives, think about how you embody each of these roles. Write down a list of things you do for each of the roles mentioned above. How can you make conscious decisions to take on even more of the wife's role?

Although men and women have different roles, marriage is designed to be complimentary and balanced as God intended. Our marriage aims to adhere to that perfect balance, and we will have harmony.

Harmony in Headship and Submission: Creating a Complimentary Marriage

At the beginning of our marriage, we had a hard time finding a balance in our roles. I had always embraced the principle of husbands taking on that leadership role within a marriage, but I couldn't fully submit to it. At times, I interrupted and tried to lead in certain aspects.

I was getting in the way of the very thing that I believed. It wasn't until we both started praying and spending time with God in the word, particularly about headship and submission, that we began to understand how our relationship was indeed supposed to reflect the love and respect Christ modeled.

Mutual love and respect are what lead you to understand headship and submission. The Bible reminds us in Ephesians 5:21, *"Submit to one another out of reverence for Christ."* Submission is not domination but mutual love, care, and respect, as demonstrated by Christ himself through his life and redemptive sacrifice.

The world so often misinterprets this beautiful biblical principle that it's blurred to seem more like losing one's voice or passivity. But the truth is that God's design for submission is far from that. 1 Peter 3:1-4 shows that submission is about trust, strength, and partnership.

Actual biblical submission does not lead you to become silent and invisible. It speaks to the quiet strength yielded when one believes in and trusts God and their spouse. You will eventually come to understand that submission is an act of faith. This will be the belief that when you respect and support your husband, you reflect gentleness, respect, and inner beauty, which God wants you to have.

A beautiful marriage can be attained only when headship and submission come together in harmony, which reflects Christ's love for the church. The only difficulty lies in finding this harmony. These principles may seem difficult at first because of the fall of man (Genesis 3). Sin distorts what God intended for good. Frequent viewing of the misuse of headship or submission can lead us to question the value and validity of God's original design. Therefore, it is wise for us to go back to the blueprint of God's design to understand the original purpose of these two principles (Beyer, 2018).

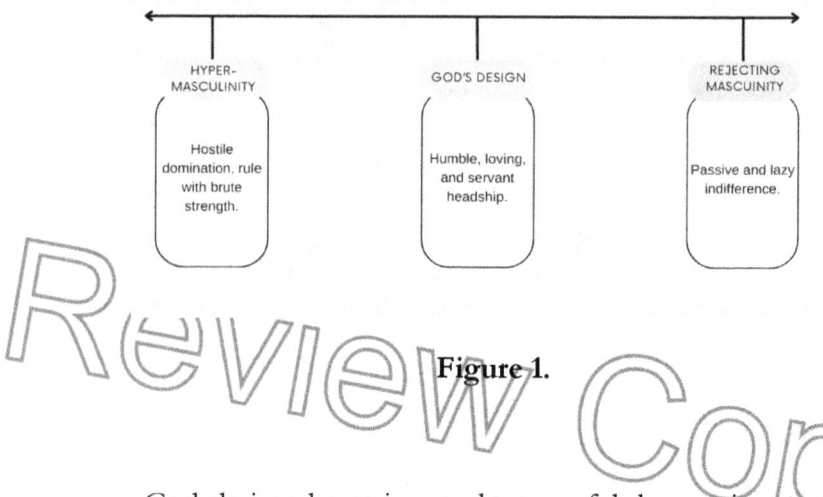

Figure 1.

God designed marriage to be peaceful, harmonious, and complimentary between the different roles of husbands and wives. We were created to have distinct roles within a marriage to balance and support each other, but sin has distorted the view of God's purpose. Making submission and headship sound like foreign concepts when, in reality, it is the perfect, godly way a marriage should be. One of the consequences of the fall was that men should rule over women. In the figure above modeled (Beyer, 2018), sin distorts the humble, loving, and servant headship into one of two extremes. Some men will reject masculinity and become passive, lazy, or indifferent, and other men will be hostile and try to dominate with strength.

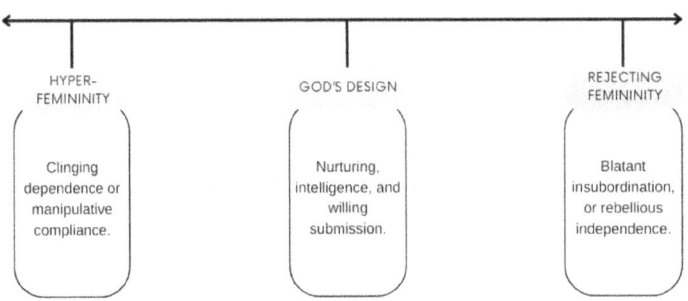

HYPER-FEMININITY	GOD'S DESIGN	REJECTING FEMININITY
Clinging dependence or manipulative compliance.	Nurturing, intelligence, and willing submission.	Blatant insubordination, or rebellious independence.

Figure 2.

Another consequence of the fall, as shown in the above diagram, is that sin distorts women's nurturing, intelligence, and willing submission. Some women will reject femininity altogether, associating submission as a bad thing and becoming rebellious and overly independent. Other women will become hyper-feminine and have a clinging dependency or become manipulative over their spouse. However, with hope and faith in the Lord, these roles within our marriage can be restored, creating a complementary balance that will result in a peaceful marriage.

With a husband leading with sacrificial love and a wife supporting him with trust, the relationship fits into the beauty of God's design. It is not about control or silence but about two people who serve one another with the heart of Christ, loving selflessly, deeply, and graciously. These two principles come together to create a complementary marriage. While complementarity acknowledges that husbands and wives may have different roles within the marriage, it does not imply a rigid hierarchy or inequality. Instead, it emphasizes shared responsibilities based on mutual respect, love, and understanding. Both spouses are called to support and complement each other in their respective roles as partners, parents, providers, and caregivers.

Likewise, husbands, live with your wives in an understanding way, showing honor to the woman as the weaker vessel since they are heirs with you of the grace of life.

— 1 Peter 3:7

When we realized our situation would change once we started following the course of headship and submission with mutual respect and service. Phelipe began to see himself as a servant rather than a leader to my needs, and I began to trust his leadership because it was founded in love.

Serving Each Other in Love: The Secret to a Happy Marriage

A selfless marriage thrives on mutual service. Philippians 2:3-4 reminds us to "do nothing out of selfish ambition, but in humility value others above yourselves." When couples serve each other, they reflect God's love in action.

I've seen this in my marriage. When my husband and I intentionally serve each other, whether it's through small acts of kindness or in more significant ways, our love extends further.

Overcoming selfishness is the key to establishing a healthy and happy marriage. A relationship where both parties focus on serving their spouse instead of themselves forms a space for love and respect to thrive.

My husband and I meditate on this daily and strive to be each other's biggest supporters, looking for ways to give rather than take. We want harmony and peace within our marriage while each takes on our roles. We can only have this by keeping Christ at the center of our marriage.

CHAPTER 3

The Covenant of Marriage

Marriage is a covenant, reflecting the eternal bond of love and unity between Christ and the Church. It is not just a transitory agreement but rather a lifelong engagement sustained by faith, commitment, and God's grace. It is the most crucial relationship after God; it is your most important earthly relationship.

The sacred bond of marriage is united by shared faith, mutual respect, forgiveness, and the strength to be derived from putting Christ at its center. With love, humility, and a choice to stand firm in the covenant under all seasons, this journey becomes full of purpose, faithfulness, and divine grace.

When we look at the marriage instituted between Adam and Eve, we see the beautiful blueprint of God's design for marriage. That was never meant to be a partnership of convenience or a contractual arrangement. No, marriage is intended to mirror something far more significant—Christ's love for the Church, a love that is sacrificial, selfless, and eternal. In Genesis 2:24, it is written:

Therefore, a man shall leave his father and mother and cleave unto his wife, and they shall be one flesh.

— Genesis 2:24

It speaks of a great truth of marital union - to leave your old and become one with another in a new, unbroken bond. Like Christ is one with His Church, we are called upon to be one with our spouse. This oneness must be expressed in the body, heart, soul, and the purpose of God Himself. This harmony lays the foundation for a promise that isn't fleeting but meant to ride through all seasons.

As relationships can easily drift apart, God's vision for marriage shines as a symbol of permanence. It's meant to endure, reflecting God's steadfast love for us—a love that never falters. Standing before God on our wedding day, we are doing far more than just exchanging rings; we are entering into a sacred commitment that mirrors God's eternal promises. This promise is not to be lightly made, and Mark 10:9 reminds us: *"Therefore, what God has joined together is that let no one separate."* You might hear marriage can just be thrown out the window during rough times, but God calls us to something greater - a love that endures every season, just as His love for us will endure for eternity. As He never turns His back on us, we are called to hold firm to our marriages in the good and the bad, confident His grace will carry us through.

Sacred Vows Before God

When two people stand at the altar with family and friends, they promise each other more than words. These vows are sacred promises made in the presence of God. A vow of love, honor, and commitment surpasses a legal contract or society's expectations.

"When you make a vow to God, do not delay to fulfill it...It is better not to make a vow than to make one and not fulfill it."

37

Our wedding vows are both a tradition and a promise binding upon our lives, as they reveal God's covenant with His people. The bond with our spouse is renewed again as we reaffirm our commitment to God, trusting Him to lead us through and sustain us in all the challenges and joys that marriage brings.

Christ at the Center: Strengthening the Bond

The strength of a marriage at its very center is anchored and held together by Christ, who anchors us through turmoil so the bond never breaks. If he's left out, relationships can quickly become frail, becoming the casualty of the pressures of life and struggling times.

And when we invite God into the heart of our marriage, He becomes the reason that keeps it from breaking; He fills in the gaps because where we fall short, grace and love fill in the absence of human effort. Any problems that we encounter in our marriage are symptoms. The actual issues are in our relationships with Christ. The relationships with our spouses begin to suffer because of something wrong with our relationship with Christ. In my marriage, the problem looked like I did not have the time or care to spend enough romantic time with my husband. The problem was that I wasn't spending enough time in the Word and not listening to what Christ commands of wives. My marriage improved as I spent more time reading my bible and trusting in what the word of God says about wives and their roles. My husband and I fought less, and we became more at peace. I can genuinely say my marriage now is the best it has been, all because God remains at the center.

The marital union wasn't meant to be carried on our own strength. When Christ is the foundation, we then discover that our love for each other deepens, our unity becomes stronger, and that which was once broken into pieces now becomes unbreakable because the hands of God Himself hold it together.

The Biblical Blueprint for a Lasting Marriage

Marriage is more than a promise or shared life—it is a partnership crafted to reflect God's love, built on commitment, respect, and faithfulness. The biblical blueprint is based on biblical foundations of a marriage that can weather any storm, where love and respect work together as the heartbeat and rhythm of unity, where forgiveness and grace heal, and where faithfulness anchors a lifelong bond, revealing God's design for a lasting, joyful union.

Love constitutes the heart of every Christ-centered marriage, not just any love, but a love that reflects Christ's love for us. It's not that passing feeling but a steadfast commitment to care, nurture, and sacrifice for one another. What does true love look like? We are reminded in 1 Corinthians 13:4-5,

"Love is patient, love is kind. It does not envy, it does not boast, it is not proud. It does not dishonor others, it is not self-seeking, it is not easily angered, it keeps no record of wrongs."

This beautiful passage lets you understand love in the way husbands should love their wives in marriage. Couples build a firm foundation that reflects sacrificial, abiding love by truly adopting these qualities.

Mutual Respect and Honor: The Heartbeat of Marriage

When you're in marriage, love and respect go hand in hand with each other. While the heartbeat of marriage is love, respect forms the rhythm that keeps a marriage healthy, just as a rhythm determines its strength in music. Here is what Ephesians 5:33 says on this balance:

However, each one of you also must love his wife as he loves himself, and the wife must respect her husband."

When a man loves his wife sacrificially and a wife respects her husband, they create the foundation of honor and mutual appreciation. This balance leads to harmonization and prevents misunderstandings from becoming prolonged conflicts.

Mutual respect allows the couple to feel appreciated and valued, making the relationship a source of joy and strength.

Becoming One: The Power of Unity

Marriage can be much more than sharing your life: it is based on becoming one with the person who is meant for you. This is well illustrated in Genesis 2:24, where the depth of the unity is expressed in saying:

"Therefore, a man shall leave his father and his mother and hold fast to his wife, and they shall become one flesh."

This unity is not only physical but also emotional and spiritual. Being one implies sharing one's dreams, fears, and burdens with another. It's about walking through life as partners, supporting each other in the good and bad, and even becoming a reflection of Christ's unity with the Church.

Forgiveness and Grace: The Glue of Marriage

No marriage is without its trials. We are human and hurt each other—sometimes intentionally, many times unintentionally. But during those moments, forgiveness is the glue that holds a marriage together.

"Bear with each other and forgive one another if any of you has a grievance against someone. Forgive as the Lord forgave you."

— Colossians 3:13

Forgiveness reflects God's grace toward us. When we choose to forgive our spouse, we welcome divine grace. Forgiveness heals past hurts, rebuilds trust, and strengthens the bond between husband and wife.

Faithfulness: Covenant of Commitment

Faithfulness is the heart of an enduring marriage. In Proverbs 5:18-19, we are called to cherish and be faithful to our spouse with such notable verses as follows.

"Rejoice in the wife of your youth. May her breasts satisfy you always, and may you ever be intoxicated with her love." This passage reminds us of the joy and satisfaction of a faithful, loving relationship. Commitment has been taken for granted, but faithfulness is the rock that keeps marriage solid even when trials come.

41

The Lifeline of a Thriving Marriage

Once you become closer to Christ and lean on his path, you will find, like I did, that praying is the lifeblood of a healthy marriage. Couples praying for each other invite God into the heart of their relationship.

"Where two or three gather in my name, there am I with them."

— **Matthew 18:19-20**

Collective prayer strengthens the spiritual relationship between partners and aligns their hearts to God's will, thus fostering unity and understanding. You can't escape the hurdles even when leading a healthy marriage. Conflict is inevitable between any two individuals, but prayer can give them the outlet toward resolution. Philippians 4:6 says, *"Do not be anxious about anything, but present your requests to God."* When couples pray to God during conflict, they find peace, clarity, and the strength to overcome obstacles together.

Building a consistent prayer routine as a couple is vital in maintaining a strong marriage. Regular communication with God keeps the husband and wife close to each other, whether it be morning devotions, evening prayers, or spontaneous moments of gratitude. In praying, couples are reminded that their marriage is a divine covenant held together by God rather than merely a human contract.

As we wrap up this look at this biblical blueprint for a lasting marriage, take some time with your spouse and consider this: How are you and your spouse embodying love that goes beyond feelings, rooted in patience, kindness, and sacrifice? Do you cultivate respect in your marriage—a rhythm of honor and appreciation that uplifts you both? Finally, in moments of challenge, how do you rely on forgiveness, faithfulness, and prayer to stay united, reflecting Christ's commitment to His Church?

This journey of marriage asks us to embrace unity not just in sharing life but in becoming one, deeply bonded in purpose, hope, and devotion. May these questions inspire you to reflect on your path, strengthening the foundation of love, respect, and faithfulness that makes a marriage enduring and flourishing.

CHAPTER 4

Laying a Solid Foundation in the Early Years

The first years of marriage can be a joyful yet challenging journey as couples navigate the complex landscape of their expectations and roles. These formative years lay the groundwork for lasting habits and patterns in communication, trust, and mutual respect. This chapter explores essential tools for building a Christ-centered marriage in those early years of marriage, from fostering open communication to finding strength in mutual submission. With biblical wisdom, real-life examples, and practical guidance, you'll discover ways to cultivate a partnership where love, respect, and faith guide you through every season.

Navigating Expectations in the Early Years

The early years are so full of joy, sometimes surprising us with unexpected challenges. When it comes to marital tension among couples in their formative years, one of the most deleterious factors is unmet expectations.

When couples enter marriage with preconceived notions about how things will be done, misunderstandings may arise.

As Proverbs 15:1 so soberly states, *"A gentle answer turns away wrath, but a harsh word stirs up anger."*

Couples can use a gentle approach to avoid unnecessary conflict and better understand each other. Instead of merely assuming what the other is supposed to do or say, it's more necessary to open up about what each is expecting from the other and set the groundwork for mutual respect at the beginning.

As an exercise, review the questions below with your spouse to discuss your expectations for each other in this marriage.

1. What expectations did you bring into marriage about daily responsibilities, communication, and shared decision-making? How might these expectations align—or differ—from your partner's?

2. Are there areas where unmet expectations have caused tension in your relationship? What gentle, honest conversation could help you bridge this gap?

3. What assumptions do you hold about your partner's role or responsibilities in the marriage? Have you openly shared these expectations, or are they unspoken?

4. What specific practices can you and your spouse implement to foster open dialogue about your expectations as they resolve?

5. How can you create a safe, respectful environment where you and your spouse can express your expectations without fear of judgment?

6. What qualities or habits can you cultivate in yourself to meet your spouse's needs and build a marriage rooted in trust, respect, and open communication?

Building Healthy Communication Patterns

Communication styles established in the first years of marriage can set the tone for the rest of the relationship. Healthy patterns of communication, such as speaking kindly, listening patiently, and making sure that the other partner has a say, establish this relationship foundation. God calls us to listen with empathy, not just to the words but also to the heart behind them. In James 1:19, there is profound wisdom for all of us in our relationships.

"Everyone should be quick to listen, slow to speak, and slow to become angry."

Intentional listening opens our hearts to emotional closeness and fosters more profound understanding. Furthermore, it lets our spouse know that we care about their thoughts and feelings, so the conversation becomes an opportunity to connect with them daily.

While listening is important, so is the ability to speak of your needs in love. Silent expectations too often result in frustration, while speaking of those wants evades tension and conflict. Whenever we speak from a place of love rather than accusation, we invite open ears rather than defensive ones. When we feel angry and look to God for patience and grace to speak our needs, we don't end up hurting anybody.

In our first year of marriage, Phelipe and I struggled to communicate. Phelipe would often be quick to get angry when certain expectations were not met. I usually responded with sharp words, and soon, our home felt more like a battleground than a haven. After a particularly intense argument, Phelipe suggested we begin praying together over our marriage, a habit we'd let slip since our wedding. Though hesitant, I agreed, and we began ending each day with a simple prayer for patience, kindness, and strength.

Over the next few weeks, our efforts started to bear fruit. Phelipe would catch himself before reacting and remembered to breathe, and I softened my tone, responding with gentleness. Each moment of intentional communication and small act of grace helped restore the love we'd almost lost. Our home gradually became a place of peace where we could embrace our differences with understanding and rediscover the warmth that had first brought us together.

Effective communication is crucial for a healthy marriage, and the Bible offers several scriptures that emphasize the importance of communication in relationships. Take your time and meditate on the following verses:

"The tongue has the power of life and death, and those who love it will eat its fruit."

— Proverbs 18:21

This verse highlights the significant impact of words on relationships. It underscores the importance of using our words wisely and speaking life into our marriages through positive and constructive communication.

"Do not let any unwholesome talk come out of your mouths, but only what is helpful for building others up according to their needs, that it may benefit those who listen."

— Ephesians 4:29

Paul encourages believers to use their words to build up and encourage others. This principle also applies to marriage, emphasizing the importance of speaking in a way that promotes unity, understanding, and edification within the relationship.

"A gentle answer turns away wrath, but a harsh word stirs up anger"

—Proverbs 15:1

This verse highlights the power of gentleness and tact in communication. It teaches that responding to conflict or disagreement with gentleness and humility can defuse tension and promote harmony within the marriage.

"My dear brothers and sisters, take note of this: Everyone should be quick to listen, slow to speak, and slow to become angry."

— James 1:19

James encourages believers to be attentive listeners and to be slow to speak in conflict or disagreement. This principle is foundational in effective communication within marriage, emphasizing the importance of listening with empathy and patience.

"The words of the reckless pierce like swords, but the tongue of the wise brings healing."

— Proverbs 12:18

This verse contrasts the destructive power of reckless words with the healing effect of wise and thoughtful

communication. It emphasizes the role of communication in fostering emotional healing and reconciliation within marriage.

By applying these biblical principles of communication—speaking life, building up, being gentle, listening attentively, and speaking wisely—couples can cultivate an environment of trust, understanding, and love within their marriage, leading to greater intimacy and harmony. Such communication prioritizes open discussion early, avoiding the pitfalls of resentment or frustration later. Whether it's a quick daily check-in or addressing deeper concerns, being intentional in communication fosters long-term understanding and peace.

Resolution of Conflicts with God's Grace

When two people come together, live under one roof, and spend every moment together, they're bound to have conflicts, yet they do not have to be destructive. Couples can turn every argument into something for growth in both spiritual and relational aspects of life. All arguments present the chance to know each other more intimately and grow in love, grace, and patience. Conflict is inevitable in marriage, but how we approach it can transform how we connect with our spouse. While emotions may run high, taking time for regular, honest check-ins creates a foundation of understanding and empathy that sustains a strong bond through life's challenges. As we learn to handle disagreements with humility, leaning on God's wisdom and seeking peace over being right, we open the door to genuine reconciliation and deepen our commitment to one another.

One way to prevent problems from coming about is through continuous check-ins on emotions. These intentional and heartfelt discussions make one openly share their feelings, and the emotional bond will never falter. These check-ins encourage mutual understanding between both spouses, for they feel loved and supported in the daily journey of life. Take time with your spouse daily to discuss how you are feeling.

No matter how often we check in with each other, conflict is inevitable. When disagreements arise, our first impulse is usually to prove we're right. However, God calls us to respond humbly, choosing His wisdom over our pride. Romans 12:18 reminds us, *"If it is possible, as far as it depends on you, live at peace with everyone."* When we humble ourselves, we open the door to reconciliation, allowing God's grace to shape our response and bring peace. Rather than seeking revenge, we're encouraged to release that desire to God; as Romans 12:19 says, "Dear friends, never take revenge. Leave that to the righteous anger of God." Letting go and entrusting our hurt to Him allows space for God's healing and guidance. Through prayer, we invite Him to bring resolution and renewal to our relationship, trusting that His wisdom will bring us closer to understanding and peace.

Once we have our response, remember to speak gently to each other. One of the worst things we can do is lose our temper and say things before calming down and thinking. Seattle Christian Counseling says when we "give ourselves over to fully venting our anger, we expose ourselves to thinking, speaking, and acting foolishly. Instead, take a timeout. Breathe. As soon as you become aware of your anger, take some intentional steps to slow down and stay engaged with your spouse to promote successful conflict resolution."

Focus on the positive aspects of your marriage and your spouse's positive traits, and communicate those to each other encouragingly (Seattle Christian Counseling). When we do this, we reassure our spouse of our love for them even though we are in the midst of conflict. Starting with a positive affirmation before bringing an issue to light can often lead the conversation positively and diffuse any conflict before it can begin.

When Phelipe and I married, I knew we would face ups and downs, but no one told me just how important it would be to focus on the good when times got tough. One evening, as we sat across from each other at the kitchen table, I found myself in a familiar spiral: I was upset that Phelipe had to keep working late to advance his career while taking college classes, and Phelipe felt unappreciated for the effort he was putting into his career. Tension thickened between us, and I could feel frustration rising. But just as I was about to snap, he remembered the advice he once read as a part of our couple devotionals we had been reading—start with the good.

Taking a deep breath, Phelipe looked at me and said, "I appreciate how supportive you've been with everything going on at work, even when it means I'm not always around." I softened, feeling seen, and replied, "And I know how much you do to keep us secure; I just miss having you here." Starting with these affirmations eased the tension between us, allowing us to talk about our feelings without anger. At that moment, we realized that highlighting each other's positive traits didn't just express love; it kept our bond strong, even in the face of conflict. Next time you must address something important to your spouse, start with a positive affirmation.

Always remember to accept each other's faults. Colossians 3:13 says, *"Bear with each other and forgive one another if any of you has a grievance against someone. Forgive as the Lord forgave you."* When we experience conflict with our spouse, we must remember that we are all imperfect. Be patient and forgive each other for our mistakes, just as Christ continually forgives us. When someone knows our faults, they really know and can love us. Sharing and accepting our faults is the foundation of love, as no one is perfect (Seattle Christian Counseling).

Sometimes, the conflicts feel so overwhelming that we cannot solve them ourselves. Outside the circle of struggle, godly counsel can bring wisdom and clarity. Whether from a trusted mentor, pastor, or counselor, outside perspectives grounded in biblical truth can help restore harmony and guide couples to a place of peace. God often uses others to help us see the path forward when we feel stuck.

This is not a marriage phase to be navigated on one's own. Proverbs teaches that *"discretion is found in those who take advice"* (Proverbs 13:10). Mentorship will enable the couple to gain wisdom from other people, keep them from pitfalls that people make, and further understand God's will for marriage.

Ultimately, a strong marriage isn't about avoiding conflict but learning to navigate it together with love and grace. By leaning into intentional check-ins, speaking gently, focusing on each other's strengths, and seeking outside counsel, we can build a foundation of trust and understanding that can withstand any storm. With God's wisdom as our guide, each challenge becomes an opportunity to grow closer, strengthening our bond and deepening the love that brought us together.

CHAPTER 5

Building Emotional, Spiritual, and Physical Intimacy

A strong, Christ-centered bond will strengthen marriage as a multidimensional connection of emotional, spiritual, and physical intimacy is formed. This chapter will discuss various forms of intimacy and explain how support between the three lays out a better partnership. From open-emotional communication to spiritual practices and even physical affection, the bonds are necessary for a healthy marriage. Through these aspects, couples can overcome their struggles together, come closer to God, and strengthen their love for each other.

In all its fullness, marriage portrays God's design for unity where emotional, spiritual, and physical intimacy come together to form a strong, enduring, and Christ-centered bond. Every type of intimacy supports and nurtures the other in building the core of a marriage that thrives through life's challenges. Just as our relationship with Christ involves different facets—love, obedience, worship—so does marriage. Couples find the richness and strength needed to flourish together in these layers of intimacy.

The Layers of Intimacy in Marriage

When contemplating the concept of intimacy in marriage, one usually focuses on one aspect: emotional intimacy, spiritual connection, or physical intimacy. However, marital intimacy is created by integrating all three.

These types of intimacy don't exist in isolation but sustain one another, just like the tree's roots, trunk, and branches work together to make it strong. The Bible gives this relationship a profound image in Ecclesiastes 4:12: *"If one overpowers him, two can resist him. A cord of three strands is not quickly broken."*

This "cord of three strands" can refer to our relationships with our spouses and God. Properly woven together, they provide a bond strong enough to withstand the pressures of life. Each strand strengthens the other so that the relationship stays resilient and deeply connected.

Emotional Intimacy: The heartbeat

When beginning with intimacy, it is vital to establish that emotional intimacy is the pulse of marriage. You share your innermost thoughts, fears, and joys with your spouse, and they, in turn, offer you a safe space to do the same. That allows us to "bear with one another in love," as instructed in Ephesians 4:2-3:

"Be completely humble and gentle; be patient, bearing with one another in love. Make every effort to keep the unity of the Spirit through the bond of peace."

Emotional intimacy comes through communication, dedicating a little time each day to talk and listen to each other. It requires empathy, letting yourself walk in your spouse's shoes to see things from their perspective.

It calls for vulnerability, letting down the guard while being open to sharing feelings, no matter how uncomfortable it may feel.

I remember a point early in my marriage when we lived on very, very thin financial margins. What was taxing for me wasn't the lack of money itself but rather the stress such financial tension was putting on our minds. We locked things up inside. We did not speak openly about our fears. When we sat down and opened up, we found peace and deepened our emotional bond.

Spiritual Intimacy: The Shared Journey of Faith

An overlooked aspect of intimacy is the presence of spiritual intimacy. Just as faith is founded on a person's relationship with God, spiritual intimacy between husband and wife is crucial for an enduring marriage. The bonding that develops through marriage in collective prayer, scripture study, and seeking God's will strengthens the bond of marriage and each partner's relationship with the Lord. Shared faith becomes an anchor at difficult times, providing direction and purpose.

Couples who constantly engage in spiritual practices together through attending church, praying, or serving others are intimate on a level that goes beyond the physical and emotional. My husband and I make it a daily routine to spend time with the Lord before sleep and during trials. Here, we can share our burdens before God, rest in His solution, and rest in each other.

Physical Intimacy: A Sacred Gift

Physical intimacy is grossly misunderstood and undervalued. But in marriage, it is a divine gift that, besides bringing joy, adds strength to the marital bond. Physical intimacy expresses love, reflecting the emotional and spiritual closeness between husband and wife.

While it's misunderstood today, sexual intimacy inside a marriage is meant to be so pure and committed that the Bible calls it a "sacred mystery," portraying God's covenant love—pure, committed, and life-giving.

It is holy: an expression of the unity between a husband and wife, made to strengthen their relationship and glorify God. Hebrews 13:4 reminds us of this sanctity: *"Marriage should be honored by all, and the marriage bed kept pure, for God will judge the adulterer and all the sexually immoral."*

Sexual intimacy in a marriage transcends just the experience of pleasure. It gives it a basis to serve God's purpose of unity and profound emotional and spiritual intimacy. It becomes an act of worship, reflecting God's unconditional love for His people if done with reverence. That's why seeing sex as a gift is highly important and to be cherished and safeguarded within the confines of a marriage.

According to Tacoma Christian Counseling, there are four principles to God-honoring sexual intimacy.

1. Sexual intimacy in marriage is for God's glory.

2. Sexual intimacy in marriage unites couples.

3. Sexual intimacy in marriage is to be other-oriented.

4. Sexual intimacy in marriage is to be regular.

Sexual intimacy is for God's glory.

Our purpose as humans is to glorify God in everything we do; it should not surprise us that this applies to sex, too. God created us with bodies. He made us in his image and with a specific gender. Genesis 1:27-28 says, *"So God created mankind in his own image, in the image of God he created them; male and female he created them. God blessed them and said, 'be fruitful and increase in number.'"* As gendered, physical beings, we reflect God's glory as we were made in His image. The apostle Paul brings this point home in his letters to the Corinthians. In 1 Corinthians 10:31, he says whether you eat or drink or whatever you do, do it all for the glory of God. That means everything we do should be about glorifying God. This includes sex.

Sexual intimacy in marriage unites couples together.

It unites husband and wife into a one-flesh relationship. Genesis 2:22-25 says, "God took part of the man's side and made a woman from the side that was taken out of the man. The man said, "This now bone of my bones and flesh of my flesh; she shall be called 'woman,' for she was taken out of man." It then says in verse 24, "That is why a man leaves his father and mother and is united to his wife, and they become one flesh." As husband and wife are joined together, they become one flesh. This intimacy between man and woman was designed to happen within a particular context. It wasn't supposed to happen between just anyone but between a man and woman committed together in a relationship with God (Tacoma Christian Counseling).

Sexual intimacy is to be other-oriented.

In 1 Corinthians: 7-4, Paul says neither spouse has authority over their own body. Their bodies belong to their spouses. Both husband and wife are to give to one another, and they are willing to yield their bodies to one another. This was a radical idea in the first century when women were thought of as only the husband's property, and even in today's society, where sex can be mainly about your own pleasure. But God created sex to be about the other person's pleasure and desires. When husbands and wives practice this principle, they take the focus off of themselves and onto their spouse's wants and desires. "When this sort of reciprocity is present, the opportunities for mutual pleasure, enjoyment, and joy are endless. When sex becomes less about what your spouse owes you and more about how you can serve your spouse, sexual intimacy is completely transformed from a mere physical act to an actual display of the gospel story" (Tacoma Christian Counseling).

Sexual intimacy is to happen regularly.

Sex glorifies God and serves as a reminder of a one-flesh relationship, so it makes sense that sexual intimacy should happen regularly. 1 Corinthians 7:2-3 says, *"A man should have sexual relations with his own wife, and each woman with her own husband. The husband should fulfill his marital duty to his wife and the wife to her husband."* It then says in 1 Corinthians 7:5, *"Do not deprive each other except perhaps by mutual consent and for a time, so that you may devote yourselves to prayer."* In this passage, Paul is instructing married couples to engage in sexual activity often to fulfill their marital duty. The activity should be consistent and never withheld from each other unless at an agreed-upon time for prayer or fasting. Paul is not explicit about the frequency or the amount of time, but it is clear that the need to engage in sexual activity is not only for pleasure and unity but to fend off temptations. Further into 1 Corinthians 7:5, Paul says, *"Then come together again so that Satan will not tempt you because of your lack of self-control."* Engaging in a healthy sex life between married couples keeps us in unity with each other while keeping our focus on our spouses and God. When our focus is on our spouse and God, it fights off the temptation of the evil one. Physical intimacy in marriage is essential. It creates a deeper intimacy between spouses and glorifies God through the union of our bodies.

To strengthen intimacy, the focus should be on keeping God at the center of your marriage through prayer and open communication between partners about their needs, fears, and boundaries. When each partner is loved enough for them to express their needs and vulnerabilities, intimacy becomes more fulfilling. Honest conversations about what works in your intimate life lead to a more satisfying relationship and build trust and emotional closeness.

Deepening Physical Intimacy

Communication is the way to develop this feature of intimacy. With honest communication, trust, affection, and passion can be rebuilt. Intimacy means more than just connection on the physical level; it stretches to connecting emotionally and spiritually, therefore loving each other more.

Couples should discuss their desires and preferences and set boundaries to ensure that physical intimacy can develop safely and lovingly. Ask yourself, is sex uniting or dividing your spouse? If your answer to that question is that sex is dividing you as a couple, go through the exercises together as a couple. Before I get into some steps that you can take to deepen physical intimacy, there are a few notes to go over:

Make a plan to thwart the real enemy.

Remember, you are both on the same team. You both want a successful, happy marriage with a fulfilling sex life. Within marriage, two individuals must be watchful of temptation because the world constantly distracts them from God's design. The temptation of lust, emotional affairs, or becoming disconnected from one's mate are all pathways the enemy uses to break up intimacy. Such temptations, however, must be met head-on in the proactive defensiveness of their hearts and minds.

My husband and I set up practical boundaries early on in our marriage: no close friendships with the opposite sex or private conversations with others that weren't shared with their spouse. We committed to praying together, asking God for protection over our marriage. Such daily surrender helped build a hedge of protection around our relationship to fend off temptation. Make it a priority to pray daily for protection over your marriage. Set time aside to pray together.

Don't blame each other.

Phelipe and I would get into some bad arguments in the early days of our marriage, and we would get angry. We wouldn't talk and make up afterward, so I often carried that anger through the night. It would sometimes last for days, with us not having any physical intimacy. We would each blame each other for the lack of sex happening, and the cycle would start again—long stretches of sexual abstinence. Things only began to get better when we decided we would pray together. We prayed for our marriage, for us to be gentler and kinder to each other, and for our sex life. Things did get better once we decided to bring it to God, but we had to work at it. Marriage is work, and nurturing your sexual intimacy takes intentional effort as well.

Make sure you are playing offense and be proactive.

You and your spouse need to work on and be proactive about building a healthy and exciting sex life. Plan a unique, romantic date night for the two of you. Phelipe and I plan a night out every couple of weeks. We are usually at home because we have two children and no close family nearby, but we set them up with a movie in the front, and we spend time in our rooms enjoying each other. We watch a movie and even play romantic couple games to build intimacy. We are also intentional with our sexual intimacy. As Juli Slattery puts it, "Making sex a priority isn't just about getting naked together. It means creating an environment that is safe and adventurous. Working on your sex life means creating time and space for conversation, relaxation, and opportunity to enjoy each other."

Now that we have reviewed some rules, try practicing the following to help deepen your physical intimacy with each other. Terry Gaspard from The Gottman Institute says the ten steps to improve intimacy are:

61

1. Change the pattern of initiating sex.

If one person is usually the pursuer, try changing up the roles. My husband usually pursues me. I have been focusing on taking the lead and initiating it more recently. It can be as simple as a look or caressing your spouse's back.

2. Hold hands more often.

Studies show that even a brief physical touch can reduce stress and create a feeling of safety as our brains release oxytocin, the "bonding hormone." Couples who hold hands often report feeling closer and more attuned to each other.

3. Allow tension to build.

True intimacy often deepens not in hurried encounters but in moments where anticipation builds, where the space between partners invites tension and connection. By slowing down and savoring these pauses, couples can transform fleeting moments into lasting memories, creating a bond that is as much about shared passion as it is about patient discovery.

4. Separate sexual intimacy from routine.

Daily life often dulls the senses, and separating sexual intimacy from routine can reinvigorate a relationship, making each encounter feel electric. Imagine a couple choosing an unfamiliar setting—perhaps the glow of a dimly lit room with soft music, far from the demands of their usual surroundings. This deliberate shift in environment and mindset allows them to explore each other with fresh curiosity, turning an ordinary night into an unforgettable experience, free from habit and rich in presence.

5. Carve out time to spend with your partner.

Intimacy often slips into the background, dulled by the hum of routines and responsibilities. But when we choose to carve out time—quiet, unhurried moments shared without distraction—we create a space where genuine connection can flourish. Take some time to plan a special dinner with your spouse. It can even be a candlelit dinner at home.

6. Focus on affectionate touch.

Affectionate touch speaks volumes without words, grounding us in the quiet language of love. Through simple, consistent gestures like the reassuring hold of a hand or a thumb caressing the back of the neck, we create a tactile rhythm that nurtures trust, breaks down barriers, and draws us closer to the one we love.

7. Practice being more emotionally available during sex.

Being emotionally open during sex means letting down your guard to share both physical pleasures and the truths of your heart. In daring to be seen this way, you build a connection beyond the physical. An honest, unscripted moment that deepens trust between you. Be willing to share your innermost wishes, fantasies, and desires with your spouse.

8. Maintain a sense of curiosity about sexual intimacy.

To foster lasting curiosity in sexual intimacy, view each moment together as part of an ongoing journey, not a destination. Asking simple questions like "What brings you joy today?" or "What do you desire right now?" can invite new levels of vulnerability, playfulness, and connection. Couples who approach intimacy with openness and wonder often deepen their bond, uncovering layers of pleasure and understanding that enrich their relationship over time.

9. Vary the kind of sex you have.

Deepening physical intimacy doesn't need to be about big, dramatic gestures. It's more about those small, meaningful changes that mix things up in the bedroom. Trying different ways to connect, whether a slow, sensual evening or a fun, spur-of-the-moment encounter, can bring back that spark and help you discover new sides of each other. My husband and I found that setting aside one night a week to try something fresh, like giving each other massages or changing up the setting, brought a renewed sense of excitement and left us feeling closer and more connected every time.

10. Make sex a priority.

In the hustle and bustle of everyday life, it's easy for work, family, and routine to overshadow the deep intimacy that keeps partners connected. However, when couples prioritize physical closeness, they build pleasure and a strong bond that enhances emotional trust. View each intimate moment as a peaceful getaway, where shared touches and vulnerability create a renewed sense of togetherness, filling you with joy and strength to face life's challenges together.

Vulnerability as Strength: The Pathway to Deeper Emotional Intimacy

In marriage, vulnerability isn't a weakness; it's the gateway to profound emotional closeness. When partners let down their guards and share their fears, dreams, and insecurities, they build a foundation of trust that strengthens over time, solidifying emotional intimacy. We will explore how choosing openness, embracing life's transitions together, and marking shared milestones can transform ordinary moments into connection anchors. In a world where authenticity is often hidden, true intimacy thrives on courage, trust, and the everyday commitment to listen and love without judgment. Here, we uncover how vulnerability, change, and celebration can deepen your emotional intimacy, revealing the beauty of a marriage built on trust and understanding.

When spouses become vulnerable, they open themselves up to creating trust that allows true closeness to blossom. While vulnerability can be viewed as a weakness for some people, it opens up deeper intimacy in marriage. Two individuals who allow themselves to drop pretenses, open their hearts up to each other, and break down the barriers of closeness and trust. Marriage should be a place where both partners feel safe to be completely honest and open. Exposing a person's fear, insecurity, and wounded past takes a lot of courage. However, it invites the spouse to see them truly, with all their faults, which allows them to love them even more.

Vulnerability draws people closer to create an even stronger emotional bond. It is the way to trust, and trust is established through actions that you do every day. It is built over time through consistent, loving actions. We don't make it by promising a lot but by following through on the small, daily commitments: showing up, being honest, and putting your spouse's needs before your own. When both act trustworthy in little things, trust builds over time organically. To foster a space of vulnerability, one must create a safe emotional space with one's partner where one does not feel threatened to open up. That is, approaching each other with compassion without being judgmental.

If we listen with kindness to our spouse's fears, dreams, and insecurities, we will create an environment of love where vulnerability can grow. Life is a transition: moving to a new city, welcoming a new member to your family, or maybe even starting a new job. Different issues arise in all seasons of life, but the opportunity to grow closer emotionally to your spouse lies within each season.

Spiritual Practices for a Deeper Connection

Spiritual intimacy is the glue that holds a Christ-centered marriage together. Common spiritual practices strengthen your relationship with God and deepen the bond between husband and wife. Including spiritual disciplines, like prayer, fasting, and meditation, in your marriage makes you grow closer as a couple. For example, agreeing to fast for a specific need, such as guidance, strength, or unity, may bring the couple closer to a more profound reliance on God and each other.

I have known many couples who prayed over important decisions, and the clarity and unity during that period tended to seal their emotional and spiritual bond. The focus of every Christ-centered marriage is embedded deeply in commitment towards prayer. Prayer aligns our hearts with God's will and brings His presence into every decision, every moment of joy, and every challenge.

When you welcome God to be at the center of your relationship, unity and strength are found, much stronger than any mortal limitation. As promised by Matthew 18:19-20: *"For where two or three gather in my name, there am I with them."*

One of the most powerful practices for keeping God's center in your marriage is through consistent, intentional prayer together. A collective setting of spiritual goals cements a journey of growth that readies and strengthens faith and unity within the marriage. It is praying together and having spiritual goals that challenge and grow your faith. This can mean committing to a daily devotion, leading a Bible study, or serving in ministry as a team. The shared goals will build purpose and unity, drawing the couple into a deeper relationship with God and one another.

Inviting God into every decision means making choices based on His wisdom, not personal desire. Within every monetary, relational, or familial decision, it often becomes necessary to seek God's will. Couples who pray over decisions regularly, asking for discernment and understanding, find peace in the hard choices. Decisions become less about what we want and more about following His perfect plan in our marriage.

In addition to the spiritual disciplines, whether in church or privately at home, worship brings a couple into God's presence. Prayer draws hearts to God and each other, setting a spiritual tone for your relationship. When couples come together to worship, they create an atmosphere of love, reverence, and unity that permeates the marriage.

Building trust and unity in marriage means investing time in nurturing all three types of intimacy—physical, emotional, and spiritual. This foundation helps create a lasting bond that can weather the inevitable challenges of any relationship.

Emotional, spiritual, and physical intimacy is part of a good marriage that lasts a lifetime. Emotional intimacy develops because, through communication and vulnerability, couples learn to care deeply for each other. Spiritual intimacy develops as couples pray together, worship, and serve others; it strengthens their marriage in faith. It is a sacrosanct expression of love. It forms the unity of marriage and is nourished by mutual respect and openness. These kinds of intimacies blended together to create a relationship that reflects God's love, holding the foundation of a partnership marked by strength, understanding, and devotion.

CHAPTER 6

Contemporary Issues in the Light of Scripture

In today's changing world, marriage can feel like driving on a bumpy road with all sorts of turns that may surprise you at any time. Each generation has unique problems, but what's happening in the current generation is unlike anything any previous generation has experienced.

Balancing two careers, social media influences, financial management, and modern family dynamics can strain a relationship. These factors are very real and demanding that they even push against the mightiest partners.

Dual Careers

Many marriages today involve two careers, each with its own sets of demands, ambitions, and sometimes conflicts. Balancing professional goals with the call of a deeply connected marriage is challenging. It is not just about handling schedules or dividing household tasks but instead fostering a bond that prospers amid modern life's pace. While many couples enjoy achieving professional dreams, these ambitions come with a conscious commitment to keeping marriage a central focus.

Mutual respect and an intentional approach are essential for a marriage to thrive alongside dual careers. During demanding schedules, have quick, frequent check-ins to discuss how you feel about balancing work and marriage. Spouses can make time for small moments of connection during a morning coffee or an evening walk. These small acts of communication keep the doors open, reminding both partners of their deep value in each other's lives. Rather than letting marriage fall to the sidelines, this intentionality keeps the relationship integrated with their shared success, making it a source of strength rather than just a background to individual achievements (Start Marriage Right).

Building a marriage that supports two careers is also built on honest, open communication. Couples discussing their upcoming demands or business trips ensure they can anticipate and adjust to each other's needs. Such proactive planning helps keep harmony even in busier seasons. I am reminded of Paul's words to the Ephesians:

"Speak the truth in love so that we will grow to become in every respect the mature body of him who is the head, that is, Christ."

70

Having an open, respectful chat about each other's needs helps build trust and keeps things clear when it matters. By talking it through, you can brainstorm ideas and make adjustments so neither of you feels stressed or overlooked. These interactions keep the relationship strong while mutual interests are pursued. Their achievements on the professional or career front are also widely appreciated. It can be as simple as attending an event at the spouse's workplace or giving support with words before a significant address.

"As iron sharpens iron, so one man sharpens another."

— Proverbs 27:17

This verse involves being each other's champion when victory is achieved and standing side by side when defeat falls. When couples support their partner's dreams, there is a shared sense of pride and unity in their marriage journey, turning individual paths into one woven with mutual respect.

When career growth is at its peak, setting boundaries around work and personal time is necessary. Set clear boundaries, and if possible, try to avoid work calls or emails during your designated "couple time." This can help both of you be present and attentive. There should be times when technology is off the table, for instance, during a family meal or an evening together, to focus on each other.

Life can get busy, so schedule date nights or downtime. Consistent time together—a dinner out or a cozy night at home—strengthens the connection. Such devoted family time is an excellent way to cultivate personal ambitions and a flourishing shared life.

Guarding Your Marriage in the Cyber Age

The act of scrolling is as much of a habit as taking a breath in the age of social media. It becomes pretty easy for marriages to slide into the subtle pitfalls of technology. With never-ending updates and a window into other people's lives, social media can easily sidetrack us from our relationships. Many couples unwittingly let screens take precedence over their spouse; without boundaries, social media can also erode the intimacy of a marriage (National University). A study published in Computers in Human Behavior found that people who do not use social media are 11 percent happier in their marriages than people who regularly use social media. Too much social media also contributes to depression and anxiety, not enough sleep, and obesity.

Another lurking danger on social media is the comparison trap. Couples can begin comparing their marriages with other perfect couples when browsing their picture-perfect life stories on social media. In reality, however, the scriptures teach us to focus our attention only on our blessings.

"Each one should test their own actions. Then they can take pride in themselves alone, without comparing themselves to someone else."

— Galatians 6:4

A grateful heart fosters contentment and gladness, guarding us from envy. Due to the issues with excessive social media use, it's important to set boundaries and place limits to maintain a healthy balance between social media and relationships.

The first step in such a relationship is setting up boundaries on social media. Simple decisions, such as avoiding eating dinner at the table with phones or defining specific "no-tech" hours, help keep precious moments together and nurture the relationship. It is that little change in refocusing our attention on each other, reminding us that what matters isn't online but right in front of us. National University recommends not keeping a separate social media life but sharing that world with your spouse. It can create a bond between you and help fight any temptations you may begin to experience if you spend all that time alone online.

In the age of social media, we need privacy and respect. Updating each other is harmless, but there are parts of the marriage that should remain private. Disagreements and intimate matters should only be discussed in the sacred space of the relationship, not in front of everyone. Private respect for each other saves the sanctity of marriage; it keeps the relationship sacred and away from the world's eyes.

Building a faithful financial foundation

One of the most sensitive areas requiring open communication is finances. Very early on, you can achieve financial unity by setting your goals and living honestly. Whether budgeting for household expenses, saving for future dreams, or discussing how to address debt, a Christ-centered marriage means a financial partnership that will be increasingly important as time passes.

This might mean discussing your short-term plans, like budgeting and debt management, while also considering your long-term plans—things like investments or retirement savings. That way, you both have a say in how the money flows and can set a direction that works for each of you. With a shared vision, couples honor God through thoughtful stewardship.

Debt management is an essential aspect of financial harmony. The Bible offers direct advice on the subject. Proverbs 22:7 says, "The borrower is a slave to the lender." The lender sets the terms of any loan, and it should be repaid with a well-thought-out plan. In this regard, a repayment plan frees individuals from financial tensions, which can quickly become stressful for relationships.

Giving and generosity are the heart of financial stewardship. As couples start planning their finances, developing a spirit of giving can deepen their relationship with one another and God. Here is what the Bible says about it:

"Command those who are rich in this present world not to be arrogant nor to put their hope in wealth, which is so uncertain, but to put their hope in God, who richly provides us with everything for our enjoyment. Command them to do good, to be rich in good deeds, and to be generous and willing to share. In this way, they will lay up treasure for themselves as a firm foundation for the coming age, so that they may take hold of the life in the way Christ intended."

—1 Timothy 6:17-19

This type of generosity encourages gratitude and the belief that your possessions are gifts to share.

Responsible saving and investing build security and are crucial to our financial discussions, which is what God wants.

74

Proverbs 21:20 says, *"The wise store up choice food and olive oil, but fools gulp theirs down."* Being wise with resources is part of honoring God and ensuring our future is stable and prepared. Similarly, Proverbs 13:11 highlights the importance of diligent savings, saying:

"Dishonest money dwindles away, but whoever gathers money little by little makes it grow."

—Proverbs 13:11

This gradual and honest accumulation reflects responsible stewardship, reminding us that careful planning honors God and our marriage. Not only do we want to save, but we also want to take what God has given us and invest in it—building a life that God has called us to live.

The Parable of the Talents, Matthew 25:14-30, reminds everyone to be wise and farsighted in managing and using their resources well. This parable starts this way: A master entrusts his wealth to three servants before going on a journey. He gives each servant a different amount of money ("talents") based on their abilities: five to one, two to another, and one to the last. The first two servants invest and double what they were given, while the third buries his talent in the ground out of fear. When the master returns, he praises the first two servants for their diligence and rewards them with greater responsibility. However, he rebukes the third servant for his inaction and lack of trust, taking away his talent and giving it to the one who has ten. The parable highlights the importance of using one's gifts responsibly, being proactive with what God entrusts to us, and avoiding fear-based inaction.

This stewardship commitment—saving and investing on purpose—ensures that the couples honor God in words and deeds by building a legacy of faithfulness and financial peace. In embracing a united vision for finances, couples steward their resources purposefully and deepen their bond and commitment to one another. Together, they prioritize values that honor God, manage debt responsibly, cultivate generosity, and plan with wisdom for the future. By aligning their financial choices with faith, couples build a legacy of trust, gratitude, and security, creating a foundation that strengthens their marriage and their shared faith journey.

Finding Unity in Blended Families

Marriage in a stepfamily brings unique challenges, such as defining your role as a stepparent, helping siblings adjust to each other, and building relationships with adult stepchildren. These complexities can make the experience more challenging than in a biological family. We will encourage you and provide tools to cultivate a loving, blended home.

There are things you want to consider before blending your family to make the transition easier. Here are ten tips to consider:

1. Define the values you want to teach your children.
2. Clarify your parenting beliefs (e.g., discipline methods).
3. Set household rules, like bedtime and screen time limits.
4. Stay committed to your parenting approach and hold each other accountable.
5. Create new family traditions to foster bonding.
6. Dedicate time for just you and your biological children.
7. Accept that a complete blend may not be achievable.

76

8. Maintain consistency to help ease transitions.
9. Speak respectfully about your ex-spouse to support your children's well-being.
10. Prepare for tough decisions along the way.

These steps can help ease the transition and strengthen family bonds before marriage. It's not easy, but you can achieve unity in your family with faithful love and firm commitment to your spouse. Ron Deal introduces the "slow cooker" or "crockpot" metaphor for blended families, emphasizing that relationships take time, often requiring years to feel like a cohesive unit. He warns against a "microwave" mentality, where couples expect quick bonding and harmony. Unrealistic expectations can lead to disappointment and feelings of failure, so patience and persistence are essential.

Establishing consistent rules and discipline is crucial for a successful blended family. While change is inevitable, maintaining stability through familiar routines and positive, consistent parenting reduces stress and pressure on children, helping them adapt more smoothly (Rawhide Youth Services). The biological parent should first handle the discipline with the step-parent's full support.

Relationship dynamics between the blended family members must be acknowledged with understanding and respect. Achieving mutual respect as an anchor fosters a feeling of importance and belonging among family members, even though there are changes in the union of two different families. Open communication and kindness can be priorities when building connections that respect each person's background while fostering a sense of unity and belonging. This creates terrific family time by creating new traditions to get the whole family together. Weekly family nights or shared celebrations create meaningful moments, strengthen your family's identity, and build lasting memories. Little and big traditions hold everything together by keeping that family commitment.

Strength and understanding grow from seeking God's guidance, primarily through life's transitions. Bringing family matters to prayer invites God's peace into the home, helping to gracefully navigate the unique challenges of blending households. This spiritual foundation fosters a loving, Christ-centered family dynamic.

Blending a family is a journey that requires patience, understanding, and a steady commitment to both your spouse and the children involved. While the challenges of navigating a new family dynamic can feel overwhelming, the tips and tools shared here provide a solid foundation for creating a loving, unified home. Remember, blending a family is not about immediate perfection—nurturing relationships, embracing change, and allowing time for bonds to grow. You can build a strong, supportive family unit that thrives over time by setting clear values, maintaining consistency, and prioritizing respect and open communication. Most importantly, lean on your faith and trust in God's guidance to bring peace, strength, and resilience to your blended family, knowing that all things are possible through His love. With patience, persistence, and a heart full of grace, you can create a home that reflects unity, love, and the beauty of coming together as one family.

Infertility and Adoption: Trust in God's Plan

This journey can be very isolating and challenging to navigate, raising issues complex to find words for, even in marriage. Longing for answers that do not come becomes an emotional burden in times of unfulfilled hope. God's Word is a comfort. He understands what we need in our most important parts and how we feel about waiting. When the path is unclear, we are invited to wait on God's timing while being assured that He works everything for our good:

"Delight yourself in the Lord, and he will give you the desires of your heart."

—Psalm 37:4

This verse calls us to seek peace and joy in God, trusting He will provide according to His perfect plan in His time. Even though waiting may seem like a long time, standing on His promise can be peaceful amid uncertainty, knowing He is near.

For some couples, God's plan for their family may involve adoption. They build a family through adoption and demonstrate God's love and acceptance. The Bible compares this to God's compassion, as He receives all of us as His children, reflecting His great mercy, much like adoption does for humans.

"The Spirit you received brought about your adoption to sonship. And by him, we cry, Father. The spirit himself testifies with our spirit that we are God's children."

Through adoption, we become instruments of God's love, giving a home and family to a child who may not have had one otherwise. It is an expression of divine love that transcends the bonds of biology, unifying families in a sacred and life-giving bond.

In waiting for new beginnings, there can be a need to find support from others. It's an encouragement and a reminder of being understood as you share your journey with the church, counseling, or small groups. When we relate to others who have gone through similar paths, we are less alone and more anchored in God's care. Such community bonds help the couple stay grounded in their faith, knowing God's love surrounds them in all seasons of life.

God leads us in all of these things, whether in times of infertility, through the process of adoption, or in the waiting periods. When we welcome His presence and believe in His way, we allow our stories, no matter how we didn't plan for them, to be those through which He demonstrates love, faithfulness, and heavenly purpose. We recall that He can bring peace in our time of waiting, remembering He is perfect in timing and faithful in fulfilling what He has placed inside us.

Marriage in today's fast-paced and changing world can get overwhelming. However, within the pages of scripture is a timeless foundation that allows couples to face their own particular challenges of life side by side. In scripture, couples find wisdom and strength in their bond together and in God. Couples who seek God's will keep their relationship ahead of world pressures and focus on things that truly matter, like building a Christ-centered home. This marriage journey will have its ups and downs, but every season of life can be an opportunity to grow in love and closeness. Steadfast in the truths of the Bible, you will find the strength and resilience to deal with any situation that arises.

CHAPTER 7

Impacting the World Through Your Marriage into the Golden Age

During each marriage season, there is a resounding call to leave a legacy far beyond our years. If a couple's love bond is anchored in faith, their love is not selfish but flows outward and reaches out to family, friends, and community to bless all of them. A God-centered marriage is a living testimony of the power of God's love for people and of perseverance, service, and unity.

In these golden years, the call deepens: how can your marriage leave an imprint that reflects God's grace?

Living in partnership isn't about enduring life's struggles but a love that will mold people and change their lives. This chapter explores how this marriage journey can influence the world and leave a lasting spiritual legacy far beyond these earthly lives.

Lifelong Growth: Deepening Your Relationship Through Faith

God-centered marriages are essentially long marriages of growth in Christ and the intimacy of walking with Him. While marriage is a union, it is also a pilgrimage of individual and conjugal faith, each urging their partner to pursue God more seriously and to rely on Him more confidently. With time, couples learn that growing together is an excellent testimony, sculpting their relationship as they reflect God's love.

"And let us consider how we may spur one another on toward love and good deeds."

— Hebrews 10:24

In a faith-based marriage, each one is challenged to support their spouse in spiritual development, to hone and nurture, for in every step forward, the couple becomes stronger individually and collectively. Encouraging growth in marriage means being the most prominent advocate for one another to seek God's wisdom. Empowering a spouse to walk his path of faith is a renewed strength that gets brought to the marriage and raises both partners while securing their bond.

Shared practices in couples' lives to deepen the relationship with God are the most important things, such as prayer, bible study, and worship. These habits become anchors of faith in everyday life while weaving God's guidance and direction. However, it is equally important to respect the different ways each of us needs to travel to come to faith. God leads His people in many ways, and sometimes, when walking with your spouse, He will nudge them one way and you another. There are times when each spouse must pursue their calling. Honoring this individuality brings richness to the marriage, a balance between shared practices and personal reflections.

Hospitality as Worship – Serving Others Together

Hospitality, at its heart, is an expression of faith—a way of opening our lives to others as God has welcomed us into His presence. In hospitality, we create space for others to experience the kindness, generosity, and warmth of God's love simply by inviting them in and caring for them.

This aspect is mainly presented as a godly deed, simply serving God Himself. When three men appeared before him, as described in Genesis 18, Abraham welcomed them and offered hospitality, recognizing the very presence of God among them. He served his guests with simple generosity and humble gestures, honoring his visitors and the God they represented. He showed humility and faithful obedience.

A marriage that welcomes hospitality as a form of faith will shine brightly within the community. When a couple serves together, it creates one purpose and gives them a shared mission, in which their bond is strengthened because they are serving Christ's love to those around them.

As they open their homes or reach out to those in need, they build a foundation of selflessness and compassion, making their relationships more profound and significant. By serving others, they are living examples of Christ's call to love each other.

"Each of you should use whatever gift you have received to serve others as faithful stewards of God's grace in its various forms."

— 1 Peter 4:10

Through this practice, couples support one another and become excellent witnesses of God's grace for all who enter their lives.

Still, even as they serve others, balance is necessary. Hospitality should never overshadow the need to nurture the marriage itself. Healthy boundaries will keep couples reserving personal time for reconnecting and recharging, maintaining a top priority on their relationship. They will thus be able to serve cheerfully and bountifully, not being made anxious by outside demands straining their marriage, with set limits around hospitality.

A Community of Faith

A Godly marriage prospers best in a supportive community of believers. Couples become much more spiritually nourished and encouraged as they intentionally seek fellowship with others who share Christian values. Such relationships are wells of support, wisdom, and accountability that help each couple grow and sustain their faith in any circumstance.

Among the most effective ways couples build these relationships is by opening their homes to friends for Bible study or small group meetings. Opening their homes to friends gives them a venue where true fellowship will be experienced and allows them to have a spiritual journey. The idea of having a Bible study isn't just immersing oneself in the Word but rather being there to pray for one another, share one's life, its victories and struggles, and remind one another of promises from God.

As they grow together, they learn more about the Word and one another. This social component of faith makes marriage a ministry of love, encouragement, and service (Family Life, 2016).

In the natural cycle of life, these friendships become especially important. Whether joyous or sorrowful, every season becomes more meaningful when shared with others who care and can offer steady guidance and support. This is beautifully said in Ecclesiastes:

"Two are better than one…if either of them falls, one can help the other up."

— Ecclesiastes 4:9-10

Bonds like these are precious in life's trying moments, giving a faith perspective that brings comfort and hope. Couples walking with other people of faith find strength in each other and the community standing beside them. The community is there not only in times of struggle but also in times of joy and rejoicing, on occasions of celebrations of anniversaries, the arrival of children, or a person's triumphs.

Through these relationships, marriage becomes a conduit for God's love, giving His grace and compassion in the lives of all it embraces. This promise of shared faith shapes their journey, leaves a strong legacy in the community, and creates a testament of unity and spiritual strength.

Building the Foundation for Lasting Legacy in the Golden Years

In building a legacy, anchoring it in faith and personal values is key. Your children and community will look to you as an example to guide their own marriages. The strength of your relationship with Christ will be reflected for others to see. As you age, keep praying and fellowshipping together; others will see your integrity, empathy, and resilience in the face of challenges. During the golden years of marriage, couples can witness the strength, grace, and devotion God has shown them throughout this journey. Your marriage will become a testimony for others. Aging naturally doesn't mean losing purpose; growing old together deepens the unity between spouses, making them a powerful reflection of God's enduring love. Every season brings a challenge to grow in gratitude for each other and their shared journey. Even the slightest shared moment will carry meaning at this stage. There's such beautiful truth in this from Psalm 92 regarding all seasons:

"They will still bear fruit in old age; they will stay fresh and green."

—Psalm 92:14

These words remind us that a marriage built on God will be fruitful and full of life even in old age. A marriage based on faith continues to change other people's lives through love, wisdom, and steadfast examples of grace.

There's often a significant change in the golden years: retirement, children leaving the house, and new care responsibilities. In these transitions, it may be scary to lean on God and each other. Still, through open communication, shared prayer, and strong faith, those are often the same transitions that strengthen us. Remember, as long as we keep our relationship strong with the Lord, our relationships with our spouse and others will continue to flourish. As we grow older, it is essential to mark milestones and create new traditions that could touch the lives of others around us. Marking milestones creates traditions and gives ways of celebrating God's faithfulness. Each anniversary, every family gathering, and every quiet moment together provide moments of gratitude. Memories written down, recorded in scrapbooks, or journals and albums build quite a tangible legacy that blesses future generations.

The most crucial factor about the later years is that they leave a legacy of faith and love. With each story shared and with each piece of wisdom passed down, couples become living examples of what it means to love and serve one another. My memories are packed with stories passed down from my grandparents about love, life, and marriage. If I ever need encouragement in my marriage, I can always turn to my grandparents for wisdom. I deeply admire and strive to emulate their long and enduring marriage. Creating a family history and sharing lessons learned with children and grandchildren solidifies the spiritual impact, inspiring others to walk in love and faith. This legacy is more than memories; it is an eternal testament to God's faithfulness, echoing through generations.

The journey of marriage will be one of movement, season after season, inviting, encouraging, and seeking to live out a calling that transcends personal happiness. In its very nature, marriage is a sacred gift and a powerful opportunity to reflect God's love and grace to the world. As couples grow together, face challenges, and embrace their golden years, they have a legacy that speaks of faith, resilience, and devotion. By loving and serving each other and others, they leave a lasting impact, reflecting God's light and reaching future generations, inspiring them to walk in faith and unity.

CHAPTER 8

Devotionals, Additional Prayers, and Exercises

Devotionals, prayers, and other spiritual activities provide the anchor to help the couple grow closer to God and each other throughout marriage. Marriage is a relationship between two individuals, but it can also become holy as they are nurtured through faith. This chapter will explain devotionals and other forms of spiritual disciplines as tools that strengthen the bond and relationship in the couples by letting their commitment to the will of God grow deeper by one's heart and will.

These practices are not habits; they are lifelines that keep us returning to God amid the noise of life. A commitment to a spiritual foundation leaves a legacy of love, unity, and faith across generations. Let's explore how couples can build their devotional life together, deepening a shared faith journey in stronger ways with every passing season.

"Therefore, encourage one another and build one another up, just as you are doing."

— **1 Thessalonians 5:11**

This sweet act of lifting one another lays a beautiful foundation for a fruitful, faith-driven marriage to flourish.

Devotions as a Couple – Growing Together Spiritually

A marriage based on spiritual growth becomes a source of strength and provides a foundation to carry on through life's ups and downs. Each grows in their walk with God and closer to the other. Such unity and strength are deeply based on faith. As it is written,

"For where two or three gather in my name, there am I with them."

—**Matthew 18:20**

As a couple involves themselves in devotionals, they open their time up to God's leading and nourishing of their relationship so that the bond between them remains strong, a base rooted in the divine. For a couple, daily devotional moments can be highly transforming. If they take time out each day, early morning or late evening, they create sacred moments that become spiritual anchors. This simple routine can help the couple begin or end their day with God's guidance to align their hearts and intentions. Even a short devotional can help a couple strengthen their spiritual journey as faith is interwoven into the relationship. Such moments are personal and shared experiences with God that bridge the partners together.

The choice of devotionals should resonate with both partners. Whether it is marriage, family, or individual growth, scripture-based devotionals can allow couples to learn about what is relevant in their current journey. Some might find a devotional that brings out the struggles and the joys of marriage, while others might focus on the general faith journeys and use it to keep themselves aligned with God's will. Thus, devotionals that bring them closer to God and each other help maintain their hearts' focus on faith and mutual support.

A practical devotional practice is crucial to making this habit sustainable. It could be setting aside a regular time—maybe over morning coffee or just before bed—to foster an everyday connection. It should be something in their shared spiritual life. This simple discipline reinforces continuity and that sense of daily renewal.

However, devotional practice is not without its challenges. With the demands of life—work, family, and social commitments—it can be challenging to have consistent time for devotion because of time constraints and varying schedules.

However, even on the busiest days, devotions as short as five or ten minutes can be incredibly spiritually productive. Couples might consider shorter devotionals when pressed for time or dividing longer devotionals into smaller, manageable parts to stay engaged even on hectic days.

Strengthening Your Union Through Prayer

A marriage based on faith has its rock in prayer. Two hearts banded together in prayer create a foundation for sustaining their union. A committed prayer practice helps their thoughts, intentions, and hopes align with God's mind, giving this union a sense of higher purpose.

Through a constant prayer life, a couple can seek God's guidance, and the marriage will be blessed with the warmth of His presence in their lives every day (Fletcher, 2024). Any form of prayer will do, but consistency deepens that bond. Couples who begin to create a routine of worship together invite God into their conversations and decisions, helping them listen with compassion, speak with patience, and act with wisdom.

A simple prayer each morning or evening may set a peaceful tone for the day or bring closure and gratitude at night. Such moments of unity through prayers, no matter how brief, help couples feel appreciated, heard, and connected not just to each other but also to God.

In intercessory prayer, one spouse prays over the other's specific needs, goals, and struggles to support and love each other. This might include a husband praying for his wife's wisdom or praying for God to strengthen her work on the job. Praying for each other fosters trust and unity as the couple reminds each other that they are seen and valued in their individual and shared journey.

In addition to the intercession prayers, couples can adopt the culture of thanking God for their blessings. A regular practice of thanksgiving prayer is a gentle yet powerful way to cultivate a spirit of gratitude, which is essential in a thriving marriage. Couples can take a moment together to thank God for their marriage and the small and large blessings they experience as individuals and as a team. Gratitude transforms hard-won victories into something divine, calling people to remember that all these victories are because of God.

"Do not be anxious about anything, but in every situation, by prayer and petition, with thanksgiving, present your requests to God. And the peace of God, which transcends all understanding, will guard your hearts and your minds in Christ Jesus."

— Philippians 4:6-7

When life goes haywire, couples are urged to seek help in God's peace by praying through these moments with their strength in Him and each other. Comfort between husband and wife allows them to let go of their anxiety and embrace a divine peace that holds their hearts steady during the most challenging times.

Prayer remains a steady foundation through every season of life. When couples intentionally build a rhythm of worship, they invite God to lead their marriage and are constantly reminded that their love story is woven into a greater divine plan.

Bible Study Exercises for Couples

It allows couples to anchor their relationship upon God's truth, cultivating unity as they align their hearts and minds to His will. Bible study combines personal and shared experiences with scripture, enabling the individual and the unified pair to find God's plans.

As iron sharpens iron, the word of God learned together presents an opportunity for each to grow and encourage one another to open their hearts for better mutual understanding and God's guidance through life.

They can start with specific themes or books of the Bible that resonate with the season or circumstances. For instance, studying themes such as patience, forgiveness, faith, or love can help them understand relevant insights into everyday challenges and joys. These scriptural themes help the couple see how God's wisdom directly applies to their lives. By choosing these themes intentionally, they let the Word become a powerful tool for growth, giving them strength and guidance for whatever season they are in. Discussing how the teachings might be applied in everyday living makes the scripture more than a study but an influence in their marriage.

Another meaningful contribution would be journaling together. Keeping a joint journal is a beautiful way for couples to record their thoughts, prayers, and reflections during each Bible study. Over time, they see the answers to their prayers and the lessons they have learned.

Proverbs declares, "The wisdom of the prudent is to give thought to their ways" (Proverbs 14:8). Beyond reflection, Bible study testifies to God's work in their lives, helping them see His guidance and favor in their journey together. These steps include selecting meaningful themes, structured study, and journaling reflections. Bible study becomes a grounding force in helping couples deepen their love and understanding in the light of God's word.

Spiritual growth is ongoing in marriages, and this makes them grow. Devotionals, prayer, and gratitude create a resilient bond that pulls the couple closer to each other and closer to God.

Conclusion

A Christ-centered marriage is a beacon of change in rewriting relationships with stability, purpose, and strength. When couples make Christ the center of their relationship, they build a connection that not only weathers life's storms but learns to thrive under them. It doesn't just happen overnight but is a journey toward mutual submission, selfless love, and servant-heartedness, all modeled perfectly by Jesus.

Mutual submission encourages both partners to prioritize each other as they develop humility and grace. Sacrificial love is identified as an example of selflessness seen in Christ's ultimate sacrifice for the Church.

Last, being servant-hearted inspires married couples daily to serve one another so their union strengthens in imitating God's unconditional love. The principles are not abstract: couples I shared the stories of in this book lived them. Their stories reveal how learning to believe in Christ brings order out of chaos, peace out of conflict, and hope out of despair. Every testimony reminds us that this transformation is a process—giving up your relationship with God one moment at a time.

But transformation doesn't happen in isolation. Contemporary marriages face unprecedented challenges—dual careers, social media, and blended families. These realities can seem overwhelming, but timeless wisdom in scripture sheds light and directs the way. For instance, when career goals are aligned with shared values, professional ambitions are the source of partnership, not tension.

Appropriate boundaries around technology safeguard intimacy and keep matters at hand. However, practical steps such as creating family traditions or practicing open communication, as in this book, remind one that the principles of the Bible are still profoundly relevant despite the changes that have occurred over the ages.

Communication is at the center of it all. Without communication, misunderstandings breed, and minor issues can grow into significant conflicts. Effective communication, as learned, begins with listening, which requires humility and sympathy. Couples approach disagreements with a prayerful heart, creating a space for reconciliation rather than division.

Strategies such as "I" statements, for example, calm dialogue, can turn conflicted moments into opportunities for growth as they deepen, strengthening the marital bond in deepening communication. That marriage relationship fosters open and honest communication, thus instilling trust and understanding between the couple.

An understanding of roles also marks godly marriage articulated in scripture but sadly misunderstood by society as hierarchical. However, scripture sketches out balance and complementarity in articulating the roles. Husbands are called to lead in love and sacrificial service, following Christ's example. Their wives are encouraged to support them with graciousness and wisdom. Such roles, when submitted to with mutual respect, cultivate harmony and purpose. Instead, they strengthen each other to flourish in their unique gifts and add a testament of Christ's union with the Church to their marriage. In accepting these roles, the couple manifests the beauty of partnership that recommends God's plan.

Marriage by Christ is never easy, but it is only through such challenges that couples learn. Whether it's stewardship in our finances, mental health concerns, or a need to reconnect emotionally, the answers in these pages remind us that the word of God gives us an apparent map for how to engage with every challenge.

For instance, focusing on gratitude shifts from deficiency to overflowing plenitude; forgiveness brings healing and restoration. Each of these practices solves the immediate problem but can also seal the relationship, preparing the couples to weather future tests of faith better.

The ups and downs of modern marriage conditions are tricky to navigate, but the Scripture's direction keeps life in balance. For managing financial stewardship, battling mental health disorders, or keeping intimacy alive during demanding life events, God's word is both a ripe and fruitful source of wisdom for couples. Challenging events happen, but those are growth opportunities. Since such couples embrace the ideas put forth by Scripture, their struggles become stepping stones for a stronger and more unified bond.

Scripture calls us to confront challenges with faith and wisdom. For example, we should responsibly steward finances, as Proverbs instructs us to honor God even in resources. The encouragement to bear one another's burdens in Galatians reflects compassion. These teachings go further in providing practical solutions that transform struggles into opportunities for growth.

Ephesians' call toward purity and unity reminds couples to focus on emotional, physical, and spiritual closeness whenever intimacy becomes strained and far from perfect. As you do these steps, know that no challenge is too great when approached with God's presence and guidance. Permit this confidence to motivate you to rely on Him, knowing that His plan for your marriage is good and perfect.

Consider the power of a faith-based community where struggles and victories are shared. Not only do these connections encourage, but they also remind couples that they are not alone on this journey. Being a part of a faith-based community creates a support system reflecting the love and accountability in scripture. The time couples come together in prayer, worship, and shared experience strengthens their relationship. Such fellowship breeds growth and resilience in the face of adversity.

Every stage of marriage has its lessons and challenges. The early years are perhaps the busiest, especially when setting routines, learning to trust, and getting to know each other. Mid-life generally involves career changes, watching children grow up or get married, and caring for aging parents. Meeting these moments with a growth mindset ensures your relationship grows continuously, aligning with God's purpose. Growth is not an easy process, but through these processes, marriages flourish.

Reflecting on this book's lessons, consider the legacy your marriage can leave behind. Your love story will influence your family, community, and generations yet unborn. Acts of mentorship, service, and sharing your faith with others will ripple far beyond your circle. Imagine leading a young couple through the trenches of trying to live out faith together or volunteering to serve a cause dear to your heart. These acts of service deepen intimacy and trust - but they are also proof of Christ's love in action.

You will leave your legacy behind, but through your life and love, you inspire others to take the same stand for Christ. Let this vision motivate you to maximize each moment, honoring God in your marriage and beyond.

What's ahead is not an end but a new beginning of a lifelong commitment to developing a Christ-honoring marriage. Pray to continue seeking God's leading, growth, and grace toward one another. Marriage reflects covenantal love between God and His people through your commitment. Share your experiences and testimonies of how these principles have impacted your relationship. Your story may just be what someone else needs. Let's build a legacy in marriage that goes from generation to generation. The following pages are devotionals designed to keep you connected to God and each other. Set aside time to do these weekly, reflect, and continue strengthening your bond.

Make a Difference with Your Review

Unlock the Power of Encouragement

"Let all that you do be done in love."

The best gifts in life aren't things—they're the love, wisdom, and encouragement we share with others.

Would you help another couple seeking to strengthen their marriage through God's Word?

Our mission with God's Blueprint for Strengthening Your Marriage is to make biblical principles practical and accessible for every couple. But to reach more people, we need your help.

Most couples pick books based on reviews. Your words could be exactly what another husband or wife needs to hear to take a step toward a stronger, faith-filled marriage.

A simple review takes less than a minute, but it could do the following:

- Encourage one more couple to invite God into their relationship.

- Help one more husband and wife grow together in faith.

- Bring one more marriage the hope and wisdom found in Scripture.

To make a difference, scan the QR code below and leave a review:

Thank you for being part of this journey with us. Your kindness means more than you know!

Blessings,

B. Mitchell-Dos Santos & Phelipe Dos Santos

COUPLE DEVOTIONALS

Week 1: Laying the Groundwork for Faith

Heavenly Father, we come into Your presence with grateful hearts, inviting You to be a part of this special moment. We are so thankful for Your establishment as the cornerstone of our relationship. Help us keep strengthening the foundation of our love relationship with You. Amen.

"Unless the Lord builds the house, the builder's labor is in vain. Unless the Lord watches over the city, the guards stand watch in vain."

— Psalm 127:1

The relationship will withstand life's storms only when God is at the center of your marriage. Just as a house stands firmly on a strong foundation, God's presence brings stability and purpose to your marriage.

Phelipe and I come from very different cultural backgrounds, which has been both a beautiful blessing and a source of challenges in our marriage. Early on, we learned that even small things—like how we express emotions or handle stress—could feel worlds apart. There were moments when communication broke down, and frustration took hold because we struggled to see things from each other's perspective. It wasn't easy, especially when life threw us curveballs like Phelipe transitioning to a demanding new military role while juggling school and his online business.

During those tough times, it felt like we were speaking different languages—not just culturally but emotionally. I wanted to support him, but I didn't always know how, and he, too, was adjusting to new pressures. Yet, in the midst of it all, we leaned on our trust in God.

We turned to prayer, asking for patience, wisdom, and the ability to see each other through His eyes. We prayed together over decisions, stressful days, and even moments of miscommunication. Studying the word reminded us of God's call to love selflessly and to bear with one another in humility and grace.

Little by little, those prayers worked in our hearts. God softened us, helping us listen more deeply and approach each other with compassion instead of frustration. We learned to appreciate our differences instead of letting them divide us. I saw how much Phelipe carried on his shoulders, and he began to understand how much I longed to share in his burdens.

Now, even when challenges arise, we know that our love isn't just about us—it's about reflecting God's love. Trusting Him has helped us weather tough times and grow closer through them. It's a daily practice of choosing to see each other through His grace, and because of that, we continue to build a marriage that thrives, even amidst life's storms. Think through some times when, by leaning on God, you were able to be clear on hard decisions or at peace during an uncertain time.

Take practical steps toward keeping God at the center. It can be as easy as praying together each day. Even one simple yet sincere prayer over mealtimes or bedtime can establish a cadence in spiritual intimacy. Then, set aside one evening a week to study the word together. Choose passages about marriage, unity, or faith and discuss how the passage applies to your life. Focus on specific marriage stories, such as Abraham and Sarah, and reflect on how their faith in God overcame uncertainties. Trust that God is watching over your marriage and guiding you through every trial.

Lord, thank You for being our firm foundation. Help us make You first in every area of our marriage. Let the bonding of trust grow deeper, and as we go on, direct us further in building a relationship founded on Your love and wisdom. Amen.

Week 2: Strengthening With Gratitude

Heavenly Father, we come before You with humble hearts. Thank you for all the blessings You have poured upon us in our relationship. Teach us to appreciate this gift every single day by coming one step closer to You and closer to each other. Amen.

"Let the peace of Christ be the arbitrariness in your hearts, to which you are also called in one body, and be thankful."

— Colossians 3:15

Gratitude enables the ordinary to become extraordinary blessings. Take some quiet time to reflect on what you are thankful for most in your spouse. Is it their encouragement, sense of humor, or comforting presence during trying times? Take some time and share it with them. Your spouse wants to know that they are appreciated, and what better way to show them than to communicate all the things you are thankful for in them? Not only are these blessings but also a manifestation of God working in your union.

Think of specific blessings that have strengthened your relationship as a couple. It could be some successful joint venture, having lived through difficult times, or just one particular tender act that perhaps even today brings smiles to both your faces. Share those and recognize how they've positively impacted the happiness and durability of your marriage.

Commit this week to making a list of things for which you are thankful. Write down those blessings each day and pray over them. Place the list somewhere visible to remind you of His faithfulness and inspire continual gratitude.

Lord, thank You for the many blessings within our marriage. Please give us a spirit of gratitude, henceforth seeing Your hand in whatever we experience together. Grow thankful hearts between my husband and me, and point us back to honor You in all we do. Amen.

Week 3: Walking in Unity

Heavenly Father, we invite You into our marriage and ask for unity and understanding in all areas of our relationship. Enable us to walk in agreement, honoring You in each step we take together. Amen.

"Though one may be overpowered, two can defend themselves. A cord of three strands is not quickly broken."

— **Ecclesiastes 4:12**

This verse beautifully illustrates how unity between two people, strengthened by God as the third strand, creates an unbreakable bond capable of withstanding life's challenges. It's a reminder that marriage thrives when both partners rely on each other and invite God to be the center of their relationship. Reflect on some areas in which you feel as a couple you are aligned, such as your values, parenting style, or spiritual goals. Celebrate those strengths, knowing they are evidence that God guides and graces your marriage. Being able to recognize and appreciate shared foundations may serve to knit the bond of your relationship together and give reassurance to you in your partnership.

But there are always areas where unity is not quite complete. These may be differences of opinion about finances, decisions on family matters, or personal goals. Discuss openly and honestly, ensuring each person's feelings are considered and heard. When conflict arises, address it humbly and be willing to yield solutions.

Consider how God's wisdom can guide your decisions and pray for His intervention when there is discord. Plan an intentional activity this week that fosters unity in your relationship. This can be as simple as praying together, working on a household project, volunteering, or even walking to discuss future goals. Apart from this, shared hobbies or volunteer work will give a feeling of teamwork and purpose, reminding you that your union is a blessing to others, too.

Unity requires work and grace. It means being unselfish, being the one to say what is best for them, even though you may not want to, and the pride to say that you are wrong. As you unify decisions, values, and actions, you reflect God's design for marriage- a co-partnership that lives on understanding, compromise, and shared purpose. Allow your walk together to be a testament to His love, encouraging others to unite their relationships.

Lord, I thank You for the gift of unity in our marriage, giving us wisdom to walk through differences and graciousness to walk in harmony. Use me as an example of Your love by revealing a unified heart that opens the eyes of others to Your leading in relationships. Amen.

Week 4: Forgiveness in Marriage

Lord, we come before You and pray for a spirit of forgiveness. Enable us to free ourselves from past hurts, extend grace to each other, and get healed by Your love. May our marriage mirror the compassion You have shown us.

"Be kind and compassionate to one another, forgiving each other, just as in Christ God forgave you."

— Ephesians 4:32

Forgiveness is the ultimate expression of love, reflecting the very essence of God's grace. It is an act to free yourself of bitterness, whereby reconciliation is extended, even though it may not necessarily be merited. Reflect on why forgiveness is crucial in your marriage. It allows you to stop holding onto hurt and anger, freeing up room for healing and peace. Without forgiveness, unresolved hurt can lead to walls that block your relationship and a lack of intimacy. Is there something you're still holding onto that you need to forgive your spouse for? Think it over, speak with your spouse about it, and forgive.

Reflect on how God's forgiveness serves as our example—gracious and complete, never holding our wrongs against us but offering us a fresh start. When extended to a spouse, this mercy displays His love. Share times when forgiveness brought healing to your marriage: maybe it was a misunderstanding resolved through a sincere apology or deeper wounds that needed time and patience to heal. Acknowledge how forgiveness reinstated your relationship and faith and belief in one another.

This week, choose one thing you will do to put forgiveness into practice. Let go of an offense you have continued to hold onto with someone, reach out and give a genuine apology, or respond mercifully to a situation. Take your time and pray together now, asking God for the power to forgive as it has been done for you. Prayer changes hearts and invites God into healing, making forgiveness transformational. Forgiveness does not mean forgetting; it means releasing the hold of past hurts to make room for love and reconciliation. It is a continuous process requiring humility, patience, and God's guidance. When you extend grace toward one another, you reveal God's heart and provide a better foundation for your marriage: trust, compassion, and mutual respect.

Lord, thank You for the gift of forgiveness and Your example. You forgave us through Christ and do not hold our faults against us. Teach us to extend that same grace to one another, finding our peace in releasing the hurt. May forgiveness be daily as it heals and strengthens our love. Amen.

Week 5: Trust God for His Timing

Heavenly Father, we come before You now with a heart that asks for patience and trust in Your perfect timing. Teach us to surrender our wishes to your will, and let us trust that your plans are always for our good. Amen.

"He has made everything beautiful in its time. He has also set eternity in the human heart, yet no one can fathom what God has done from beginning to end."

— Ecclesiastes 3:11

Waiting on God is often challenging, especially when delays and unclear answers arise. In these very waits, God frequently does His deepest work in our lives. Consider how trusting God's timing has empowered your marriage. After COVID, Phelipe and I faced financial challenges, especially with the needs of our three boys—two of whom were under three. While I was grateful to have a fully remote job that allowed us to cover our bills, there wasn't much left over. We turned to prayer, trusting God to provide for our family. Over time, as we continued to lean on Him, blessings unfolded. That same year, Phelipe was accepted into officer school for the military, opening the door to increased income, and I received a promotion at work with a significant pay raise. All glory goes to God, who carried us through, even when we didn't know when relief would come.

Perhaps you experienced a time of uncertainty when you came into a place of resting in each other and in the control of God. These times remind us that His plans are more significant than our understanding and that His timing is always perfect. Take a moment to discuss areas in your marriage where you are still waiting for clarity or answers: perhaps guidance about a big decision, healing from a hurt, or prayers regarding your family's future. Share honestly as frustrations or fears are expressed, encouraging one another to stand firm in faith.

Commit yourselves to prayer in these seasons of waiting. Take the time to pray for patience and strength to trust in His plans. You may repeat specific prayers daily, looking for a way to release the uncertainties of life to Him. Remember as you pray that God's timing is not delayed but an opportunity for spiritual growth and more profound dependence upon Him.

Waiting upon God's timing is faith in action. Forgive the need to control a situation and trust His plan to work out the way and time He ordains. Lean into His promises, for He works out all things together for your good and His glory.

Lord, thank You for Your wisdom and the beauty of Your perfect timing. Help us trust Your plans, though we often can't see the whole picture. Teach us patience, deepen our faith, and guide us on a journey together in Your love. Amen.

Week 6: Serve in Love Together

Heavenly Father, we come before You today asking that You give us a servant's heart and a spirit of humility in our marriage. Enable us to serve one another in love as You have shown us the example of selflessness and grace. Amen.

"You, brothers, were called to be free. However, do not use your freedom to indulge in the flesh; rather, serve one another in love."

— **Galatians 5:13**

Serving one another in marriage speaks volumes of love and respect. This reflects Christ Himself, who, though worthy of service, came to serve. Discuss how acts of service- small or grand have deepened your bond as a couple. It may be through simple tasks associated with daily life, like making a meal or lending an ear to listen. These acts of care will nurture your relationship and honor God's design for marriage.

This week, plan to serve one another in a concrete act. It may be a tangible thing, like doing a chore that your spouse finds burdensome, or an emotional act, like writing a note to encourage. As you begin these acts of service, reflect on how loving and serving one another promotes love, humility, and gratitude.

Serving others together pushes it out of your home and into the world. Reflect upon how times of shared service—whether at church or helping out a neighbor in need—have brought you closer to one another. These build unity, reminding one that marriage is to be done in partnership to glorify God. You can be a testament to His love and compassion through your actions.

Serving is the humility to put aside your self-interest and cater to your spouse's needs. In doing this, you mirror Christ's love, making your relationship more substantial and aligned with His mindset. Let serving one another be a daily practice that enriches your marriage and brings glory to God.

Lord, thank You for calling us to serve one another in love. Help us to approach each day with a humble heart, the disposition of a servant, and the ever-active desire to raise and support each other. May our acts of service bring glory to you and deepen our love. Amen.

Heavenly Father, we come before You to receive Your peace in our hearts and homes. Enable us to be peacemakers in this marriage, reflecting Your love in what we say and do and in our decisions. May Your peace guide us in all we do. Amen.

"Peacemakers who sow in peace reap a harvest of righteousness."

— James 3:18

Marriage peace does not come from a lack of conflict but from understanding cultivated by work and grace. Conflict will be part of any relationship, but it should be resolved quickly to maintain peace. Take some time reflecting together on the areas in your marriage where tension or disagreement tends to surface. Knowing these specific areas is vital to begin sorting them out in wisdom and love, whether over finances, parenting styles, or household responsibilities. Consider how your words and actions affect your spouse in times of disagreement.

A relationship can create peace by listening to one another with compassion and empathy. In all conflicts or misunderstandings, take a minute to genuinely listen to each other without thinking about what to say in return or how to defend yourself. Active listening opens the heart and fosters understanding and respect, which can help to resolve even difficult situations. Practice responding with words that build up rather than tear down. A simple "I understand how you feel" can be a bridge to reconciliation.

Being a peacemaker requires humility and prioritizing understanding over being right. It also includes establishing an atmosphere of love and respect. Small acts of intentional caring make a big difference in your relationship. Discuss practical ways you can plant peacemaking seeds in everyday real-life interactions, such as a compliment, showing appreciation, or choosing not to react during hot emotional moments. Such actions build a sense of security and attachment, softening your relationship.

It is not limited to your house. Ponder how you might bring peace to your community. Sometimes, acts of service, encouragement, or calm in the storm can show Christ's love. And as you lead by example and model a peacemaker in your home and beyond, you will be living out His calling to sow those seeds of peace and righteousness.

This week, make a conscious choice to speak only healing, uplifting words. Inevitably, an issue will arise that could bring a response from one or both of you. Before responding, take a moment first to stop and pray. Ask God to give you the wisdom and patience to work through the conflict lovingly and understandingly. Take time this week to commit James 3:18 to memory together as a reminder of the blessings that follow from pursuing peace. Sow seeds of peace, and the harvest of righteousness you'll grow will bring stability to your marriage and honor to God.

Lord, thank You for this gift of peace that surpasses understanding. Please help us pursue harmony in our marriage and be peacemakers in our community. Guide our words and actions to reflect Your love and bring glory to Your name. Amen.

Heavenly Father, thank You for this gift of joy that's born from knowing You. Lord, fill our marriage with a spirit of gratitude and celebration. Enable us to find joy in the blessings You have given us and to share that joy with others. Amen.

"Do not grieve, for the joy of the Lord is your strength."

— Nehemiah 8:10

Joy is a fruit of the Spirit that cheers, stabilizes, and empowers us even in the worst times. It is more than happiness; it is that more profound, steady sense of contentment rooted in trusting God and seeing His goodness in everything. Reflect on the moments within your marriage that brought you joy.

Maybe these were moments when laughter was shared, you found comfort in each other's presence, or you celebrated a landmark. These are not random moments but gifts from God, reminding you of His faithfulness and love towards you as a couple and how God's joy has carried you through difficult seasons.

Remember what was happening around the time when life was overwhelming and how you found strength in trusting His plan. Perhaps it was when a financial strain, a health challenge, or a significant life transition occurred. Reflect on how leaning on each other and Him brought you not only through the difficulty but closer together.

Joy doesn't eliminate hardship; it reassures us of God's presence and promises, strengthening us to face the adversary and even thrive. This week, do a planned activity that sparks joy for both of you. It doesn't have to be significant because small moments can be joyful. That could be cooking a meal, walking, or revisiting some favorite memories by looking at old pictures and videos.

Doing things together allows you to appreciate the life you have built and reconnect with each other. Also, try to get into the habit of incorporating gratitude into your daily routine. Set aside a time at the beginning or end of each day to share one thing that delights you. This simple practice will change your perspective, focusing your heart on God's abundant blessings.

Living with joy is rejoicing in all the things God has done for you, the little and the big. Gratitude rewires your mind to look at the world from a new perspective. Instead of focusing on what you do not have, it will have you concentrate on all the blessings you already have. Reflect on how this might affect your marriage. When you view life through a lens of gratitude, joy naturally follows, and your marriage becomes a living testimony to God's provision and love.

Now, together as a couple, reflect on how to give others joy: Joy shared is joy multiplied. It might be little acts of kindness, such as helping a neighbor, sending a thoughtful note, or volunteering together. Perhaps it is as simple as offering encouragement or being a source of positivity in someone's day. It is in sharing the joy of the Lord that a couple finds bonding and reflects that light into the world. Joy is contagious, and a marriage centered on the joy of God becomes a beacon of hope and encouragement to those around them.

Lord, thank You for the great happiness that comes from knowing You and following Your ways. Cause us to live with grateful hearts and to praise Your goodness continually. May our marriage be a joy to each other and a testimony of Your goodness. Guide us to share that joy with others so they may see Your love through us. Amen.

Father, we thank You for your endless patience with us and the example of grace You have given. Please help us to clothe ourselves with compassion, kindness, humility, gentleness, and patience in our marriage. Teach us to wait on You and one another with understanding and love. Amen.

Therefore, as God's chosen people, holy and dearly loved, clothe yourselves with compassion, kindness, humility, gentleness, and patience.

— **Colossians 3:12**

Patience is a key ingredient in a successful marriage, reflecting God's character and His love toward us. Look back to those times in your marriage when patience brought peace and allowed growth. Maybe it was during a transition point in life: transitioning into parenthood, navigating career changes, or working through misunderstandings. In those moments, patience made room for healing, understanding, and mutual support.

Discuss which areas of your relationship tend to breed conflict, such as important decisions, styles of communication, or even routine things. Then, acknowledge how impatience ramps up tension and closes off the connection. Commit to small, tangible ways to practice patience, such as stopping oneself before responding in frustration and fully understanding a spouse's perspective.

For me, practicing patience is something I must remind myself to do more often than I would like. At the beginning of my marriage, I let my frustrations boil over, which usually caused Phelipe and me to fight. My approach to handling conflict was not one of patience. Some may call me a neat freak, but I love things clean. Phelipe would constantly leave dishes out and not put them away in the dishwasher, often causing fights. As time went on, I realized that if I approached things with patience and a pleasant tone, the arguments wouldn't start, and Phelipe would be more open to listening to me if I spoke to him nicely instead of through frustrations. A dish is left out occasionally, but it does not upset me; instead, I focus on everything I love about him. Remember, no one is perfect, and we must extend patience daily to our spouses. Conflicts arise, but starting from a place of patience can help curb arguments. Consider how extending patience is a reflection of God's love. Since He is slow to anger and rich in love, we must also reflect grace in our interactions. This week, identify one concrete area where impatience usually kicks in and commit to one specific response of patience and kindness. For example, if schedules get crazy, offer encouragement rather than criticism.

Pray together for grace to handle such issues lovingly and understandingly. Remember, they are a fruit of the Spirit and grow as you lean upon God. Patience also builds resilience in your relationship. It leaves room for growth and extends a degree of grace to each of you while you learn to work through imperfection together. In cultivating patience, you foster an environment of security and trust where both are valued and understood.

Lord, thank You for Your patience with us when we fall short. Teach us to extend that patience to one another and reflect your love in our marriage. May we grow in kindness, understanding, and grace together in unity and peace. Amen.

Week 10: A Marriage That Reflects Christ

Heavenly Father, we welcome You into our marriage and ask that it be a union that glorifies You and reflects Your boundless love. Teach us to love one another as You have loved us and that our relationship may draw others closer to You. Amen.

"A new command I give you: Love one another. As I have loved you, so you must love one another. By this, everyone will know that you are my disciples if you love one another."

— **John 13:34-35**

Marriage is a unique covenant relationship, encompassing the singular place to mirror Christ's love. As a couple, reflect on how your words, actions, and life reveal the heart of Christ's sacrificial and unconditional love. Consider the seasons in your marriage when your journey has powerfully demonstrated His grace—through acts of forgiveness, service, and encouragement during challenging times.

How can you model Christ's love in your relationship? It may be extending grace when misunderstandings arise, carving out time for one another in your hectic schedules, or praying together regularly. Consider also how you might take that love further and express it to others. Maybe serving hand in hand in your community, developing up-and-coming couples, or just being an active ear, your marriage has terrific potential to be a strong testament to God's love in action.

Commit to one intentional act this week that speaks volumes of Christ's love. This might be as simple as writing a love note, encouraging your spouse, serving together, or having friends or family over for a meal. In those actions of love, your heart is strengthened toward one another and glorifies God, revealing His light in the world.

Let your marriage be a living testimony to His love partnership that inspires others to seek Him. Remember, how you love and serve one another reflects Christ's love for us all.

Lord, thank You for Your infinite love that sustains and guides us. Direct our lives so we can learn to love each other humbly and graciously, even as You have set the example for us. Let our marriage honor You and be a light to point others to Your heart. Amen.

Week 11: Embracing the Challenge, Overcoming It

Lord, we come to You seeking insight and guidance regarding our challenges in this marriage. Please provide insight to identify areas where we need growth and lead us to approach each struggle with gracious and humble responses. Ultimately, may Your presence be what carries us toward healing and unity. Amen.

"Therefore, confess your sins to each other and pray for each other so that you may be healed. The prayer of a righteous person is powerful and effective."

— James 5:16

While any relationship must face challenges, how we approach them sometimes draws us closer or further apart. Reflect on the current struggles that are affecting your marriage. Are there unresolved issues, unspoken feelings, or areas of tension that need to be shared? In recognizing these issues, the first step toward overcoming them can be sought, so it is essential to be open and confess anything that may be bothering you.

Develop a safe space where open communication is fostered. Talk about how both of you need to have at least one time to be heard and valued. Consider setting aside regular time to talk without distractions, focusing most on listening with empathy rather than responding defensively. And when you approach challenges as a team, you invite God's wisdom and strength into your relationship. This week, write down one thing you must confess to your spouse (e.g., an overlooked need, hurtful words, or missed expectations). Take turns sharing and responding with grace.

Father, thank You for Your grace that holds us in our weakness. Please help us face hardships with honesty, courage, and unity. Teach us to lean on You and to approach every challenge in a spirit of love and humility. Let Your power work through us to bring healing and strength into our marriage. Amen.

Heavenly Father, we come before You with humbled hearts and pray for strength to forgive as You have forgiven us. Enabling us to extend grace and mercy toward one another so that our marriage may mirror Your love and compassion. Amen.

"Then Peter came to Jesus and asked, 'Lord, how many times shall I forgive my brother or sister who sins against me? Up to seven times?' Jesus answered, 'I tell you, not seven times, but seventy times seven."

— Matthew 18:21-22

In this verse, Jesus says there is no limit to how many times you must forgive someone. It is a limitless number. We are called to forgive repeatedly, just as Christ forgives us for all our sins. Forgiveness is crucial in our relationships as no one is perfect, and we will all make mistakes. The only way a marriage can succeed is through this act of forgiveness. Please take a minute to reflect on why it is so crucial in your marriage. Resentment or anger can build walls between two people, while forgiveness tears those walls down, opening the doorway to allow healing. Take a minute to consider how forgiveness reflects God's grace, enabling you to release your hurts and move forward together in harmony.

Share times in your marriage when forgiveness brought healing from a minor misunderstanding or a deeper wound that took time and effort to mend. Acknowledge how such experiences brought growth to you as a couple. Forgiveness is not an act of letting go but of love that reflects God's mercy and transforms relationships.

This week, share one way your spouse has shown you grace in the past.

Commit to one specific act of grace you'll offer in the coming week. And remember, forgiveness does not involve forgetting; it consists of choosing love and grace over bitterness and division.

Lord, thank You for the forgiveness You have extended to us through Christ. Help us extend that same grace to one another so our marriage may testify to Your love and mercy. Please help us to release bitterness and to rejoice in reconciliation. Amen.

Heavenly Father, we come before You with open hearts, asking for faith in Your perfect plan for our lives and marriage. Help us drop our fears and uncertainties before Your wisdom and guidance. May we proceed with confidence, knowing You are in control. Amen.

"For my thoughts are not your thoughts, neither are your ways my ways,' declares the Lord. 'As the heavens are higher than the earth, so are my ways higher than your ways and my thoughts than your thoughts."

— Isaiah 55:8-9

Life is full of uncertainties that sometimes make it difficult to trust God completely. When things do not go according to plan or while one waits seemingly forever, it is easy to panic or become defeated.

But then the Word brings us back to reality. God's thoughts and ways are well out of our grasp. Take a moment to reflect together on one of those moments when you experienced uncertainty in your relationship, went through a financial challenge, changed jobs, or were waiting for something. How could trusting in God's plan, in those moments, bring clarity or peace? Let's share some experiences that remind us of His faithfulness.

Being passive is not the same as trusting God's plan; genuine trust involves actively leaning into His promises and

129

guidance. Share areas in your marriage where you seek clarity or resolution. Are there any goals, dreams, or decisions that feel overwhelming or unclear? Take time to find where you can align these with God's will. It might be through praying for discernment, wisdom from scripture, or counsel from trusted mentors centered around faith.

It also takes humility and surrender to align your goals with God's plan. That means letting go of control and trusting that He is working for your good when the path ahead is unclear. As a couple, set time each day to pray for God's guidance. Whether it is a morning devotion or an evening prayer, these moments of connection with Him and each other reinforce your trust in His perfect timing.

This week, start with one practice that deepens your dependence on God: journaling prayers and thoughts, making a list of scriptures to focus on, or even fasting together. As you both intentionally set your eyes on Him to lead you in decisions, you will find strength and cohesion in trusting His will concerning your marriage.

Lord, we thank You for being the author of our story. Help us trust Your timing, work in peace through yielding ourselves to You, and give us the courage to step forward in faith, trusting that Your ways are perfect and Your love does not change. Align our hearts to Your will, and let our marriage be but a reflection of the beauty of trusting in You. Amen.

Heavenly Father, thank You for giving us marriage and Your plan concerning intimacy as a reflection of Your love. Create in us clean hearts and renew unyielding spirits within us. Guard our marriage, cover us from temptation, and guide us to honor You through all our actions. Amen.

"Create in me a pure heart, O God, and renew a steadfast spirit within me."

— Psalm 51:10

Purity within marriage is not one-dimensional; it's a multi-faceted commitment to all areas of life: physical, emotional, and spiritual. It means respecting each other and God enough to keep a relationship clothed in love and faithfulness. Reflect on how you have been enriched in marriage through obedience to God's design for intimacy. How has striving to give priority to purity brought you closer to each other and closer to Him?

Physical purity refers to not violating the sacredness of your union. Discuss and set boundaries and behaviors that will protect you from temptations. These could include setting boundaries on what to watch, being intentional about quality time together, or avoiding situations that could compromise them. These protections set up a safe space in which love can grow.

Emotional purity also plays an important role when it involves trust and intimacy. Think of the barriers that exist, like unresolved conflicts, unresolved insecurities, and unmet expectations, and commit yourself to working through these honestly and compassionately to develop a deeper connection and mutual understanding. Open communication is the very basis on which emotional closeness can develop.

Spiritual purity provides the foundation upon which this Christ-centered marriage must be based. Discuss how you could invite God into your relationship through prayer, Bible study, or serving together. Reflect on how these activities build your faith and the bond between them. Such actions as praying with each other every morning would give a spiritual orientation to the whole day, while scripture study brings wisdom and insight to problem-solving.

This week, do something to protect the purity of your marriage. Maybe that's a date night where you connect on an emotional level; perhaps it is promising to pray each day for protection and guidance, or you could even serve others together. Keeping purity first honors God and lays a firm foundation for your relationship.

Lord, we pray for protection over our marriage. Keep our hearts and minds pure and guard us against the temptations of this world. May our relationship reflect Your love, and let the purity of our commitment and devotion bring glory to Your name. Empower us to honor You in everything we do; restore steadfast and glorifying spirits to us. Amen.

Heavenly Father, we come before You, asking that You guide us in building deeper emotional intimacy in our marriage. Please help us to be open and supportive of each other. Teach us the art of compassionate listening and open sharing to strengthen our bond and reflect Your love. Amen.

"Therefore encourage one another and build each other up, just as, in fact, you are doing."

— 1 Thessalonians 5:11

Emotional intimacy forms the very core of a deeply connected marriage. It provides an avenue for sharing your fears, hopes, and dreams without judgment and a space where vulnerability is safely allowed. Reflect together on what might get in the way of emotional closeness. Perhaps it is some fear of rejection, hurt from the past, or unresolved conflicts. Discuss these openly, recognizing that identifying these barriers is a step toward healing.

Take concrete steps toward emotional openness. Set aside some time each week to spend with your spouse, making sure to have purposeful, uninterrupted conversations in which both of you can share your feelings. Practice active listening by repeating what your spouse has shared to understand it. Also, be sure to regularly let each other know the things you appreciate about one another; small affirmations can go a long way in building a foundation of feeling secure and trusted.

Reflect on how emotional vulnerability has strengthened your bond. Opening your heart to your spouse means allowing the other person to see your true self. This transparency deepens the connection and enforces trust in a relationship, which only a lasting one can gain. Share moments when vulnerability brought you two closer together: hard conversations, shared struggles, or acts of kindness shown.

Lord, we are grateful for emotional intimacy within marriage. Please allow us to break down the walls that separate us and approach each other with compassion and empathy. Teach us from Your example how to listen well, open our hearts, and bear one another's burdens. May our relationship blossom further as we reflect on Your love. Amen.

Week 16: Deepening Spiritual Unity

Lord, we invite You to the very center of our marriage. Enable us to draw closer to You and closer to each other through shared faith. Teach us the value of supporting one another in spiritual journeying and seeking Your guidance in every area of life. Amen.

"I am the vine; you are the branches. If you remain in me and I in you, you will bear much fruit; apart from me, you can do nothing."

— **John 15:5**

Spiritual unity serves as the backbone of a Christ-centered marriage. When both partners are rooted in faith, their bond is strengthened and prevails over anything.

Spiritual oneness does not mean your faith journeys will resemble each other. Instead, learn to respect how God uniquely works in your lives, and then strive to spur one another on in those unique paths. Share what the Lord is teaching you through prayer, scripture, or experiences, and then ask for the same from your spouse. In this mutual spurring of one another, you will live united.

Reflect on how you can practically encourage one another in your walk. You may pray for one another daily, attend a Bible study together, or serve in a particular ministry. It's these kinds of activities that will help you walk with God and with each other. Think about how the centrality of Christ in your marriage affects your decision-making, values, and what's important to you.

Commit this week to doing something together as a couple to dig deeper into your spiritual unity. That may be a devotional plan together, dedicated time to worship, or memorizing a verse that someone might identify with during that season. These deliberate efforts will create a spiritual connection to preserve and enhance your relationship.

Dear God, thank You for this gift of spiritual unity in marriage. Teach us to push ourselves toward our relationship with You as we learn that deepening the bond with You will deepen it with one another. Teach us to support one another in faith and to honor You in everything we do. May our marriage prosper as we live in You, the true vine.

God, we want to seek Your protection over our hearts and minds. Teach us to guard against negative and impure thoughts and continue to do whatever is noble and true. Create a marriage honoring You in all our thoughts, words, and deeds. Amen.

"Above all else, guard your heart, for everything you do flows from it."

— Proverbs 4:23

Taking care of your heart means caring for what you let into it. The heart determines and guides your choices and the relationships around you. Consider examples of influences—what you read, hear, and experience. Talk through how that might become an influence or burden on your relationship or an encouragement to each other.

Criticism, cynicism, or even unhealthy comparisons might poison trust and happiness in the marriage. Teach yourselves how to eliminate or avoid the negativities in your lives. Using good habits like words of affirmation, meaningful talks, and prayer will create an atmosphere of love and encouragement.

A marriage that reflects God's love has to be intentionally created in a setting where partners feel supported and valued. Speak words of encouragement every day, even when it is not easy. Appreciate each other's strengths and efforts and seek grace and understanding for each disagreement.

Take some time this week to review the influences in your life. Discuss practical ways to protect your hearts and minds, such as cutting back on social media, limiting exposure to damaging discussions, and perhaps reading scripture together. Exchange hurtful habits for encouraging ones that draw you closer to God and each other.

Lord, thank You for the wisdom of Your word in helping us guard our hearts. Help us screen out unhelpful thinking and be intent on what is pure and helpful. May our thoughts and actions be protected and help enrich an environment that testifies to Your love and grace. Amen.

Week 18: Building Gratitude Together

Heavenly Father, we thank You for the blessings poured into our lives. Teach us to cultivate hearts of gratitude even in trying times. Help us recognize and celebrate Your faithfulness as we draw closer to You and each other. Amen.

"Let the peace of Christ rule in your hearts, since as members of one body you were called to peace. And be thankful."

— Colossians 3:15

Gratitude shifts your vision from finding what is lacking to realizing the fullness of God's provision. Reflect on the blessings in your relationship—big and small—that have strengthened your bond. It could be shared memories, answered prayers, or the gift of each other's presence. Discuss how these remind you of God's goodness and care.

Consider how cultivating gratitude impacts your marriage. When you intentionally thank God for His blessings, you build a foundation of joy and contentment. Gratitude softens hard heads, allowing forgiveness, patience, and love. Share specific qualities or actions you appreciate about each other, letting these affirmations encourage and uplift your spirits.

Commit this week to practicing gratitude together. Start a gratitude journal, recording at least one blessing each day. Share these entries, pray over them, and thank God for His faithfulness. Seek ways to express gratitude outwardly, such as writing a note of thanks, speaking a kind word, or giving generously to someone in need.

Gratitude also brings your attention to His peace. Consider ways to share this atmosphere of thankfulness with others as a couple. Perhaps you could volunteer together, encourage a friend, or share a testimony of God's goodness. And as you live with thankful hearts, you're growing your marriage and inspiring others to seek His faithfulness.

Father, thank You for Your blessings. Teach us to cultivate hearts of gratitude, seeing Your hand in every season of our lives. May our marriage be a reflection of enjoying Your grace; may it reflect Your good and what others can see on it to trust Your goodness. Amen.

Heavenly Father, we seek wisdom and patience in the words we bring to each other. Give us ears that hear with compassion, mouths that speak with love, and hearts where minds live to understand each other. Our words remind us of Your loving grace and encourage us toward each other. Amen.

"Do not let any unwholesome talk come out of your mouths, but only what is helpful for building others up according to their needs, that it may benefit those who listen."

— **Ephesians 4:29**

A strong and healthy marriage is built on quality communication between the couple. Reflect together about how your words and actions impact one another. Are your conversations encouraging and constructive, or sometimes damaging to the relationship through misunderstandings or hurt feelings? Recognize that not one of us always communicates well, but very intentional small changes can be compelling.

Effective communication starts with listening skills. When one person is speaking, the other should be actively listening at the moment, free from distractions, and fully present. Reflect on moments when you felt heard and valued in your marriage. How could you recreate those moments more often?

Equally important is choosing your words wisely. Proverbs 15:1 reminds us that "a gentle answer turns away wrath, but a harsh word stirs up anger." Discuss how you can approach disagreements with kindness and respect. Consider setting aside regular times to discuss important matters, ensuring both partners feel heard and respected.

Commit to one practice that strengthens your communication. It might be pausing to pray before discussing a challenging topic, practicing "I" statements to express your feelings, or writing a thoughtful note encouraging your spouse. These small actions can build trust and foster unity.

God, we thank You for the gift of communication and the possibility of getting closer through our words. Teach us to listen with empathy and speak with kindness while building each other up according to Your will. Let our conversations honor You, and let our love grow stronger. Amen.

Dear heavenly Father, we commit our marriage to you, seeking wisdom for an enduring legacy of faith. Help us live such exemplary lives that those around us will be inspired and draw closer to You. Guide us as we strive to leave an enduring impact on Your kingdom. Amen.

"But as for me and my house, we will serve the Lord."

— **Joshua 24:15**

A Christ-centered marriage is more than a personal blessing; it is an opportunity to leave behind a spiritual legacy that will influence future generations. Reflect on how your relationship serves as a witness of God's love and faithfulness. Discuss how your actions, decisions, and values can inspire others to search for God.

Building a legacy begins at home. You could pray together and share devotional time, modeling Christ-like behavior in day-to-day life. Reflect on how to make traditions that remind them to keep faith—go to church regularly, celebrate milestones with gratitude, or volunteer together.

Beyond your family, think of how your marriage can impact your community. Are there ways you can serve together, offer encouragement to others, or even mentor younger couples? You are a light that guides people toward Christ as you live out your faith. Those small acts of kindness and consistency in walking with God can have ripples touching people beyond anything you might ever know.

Commit this week to one act that expresses your desire to leave a legacy of faith. Share the word with a family member today, pray with an ailing friend, or openly live out God's love in some way to a neighbor. Plant seeds today, and God will harvest in His own time.

Consider how your legacy will outlive you. What values and wisdom do you want to pass on to your children, grandchildren, or those around you? A Christ-centered marriage will strengthen your relationship and become a testament of faith that lives on long after the couple's passing.

Lord, thank You for this opportunity to build a legacy that will be a source of praise for You. May our lives clearly and consistently testify that people can trust in You. Let our marriage point others toward Your love and faithfulness for us. Amen.

Week 21: Building Your Relationship on a Solid Foundation

Thank You, God, for Your ever-present presence and for bringing us together. We ask for guidance as we look to continue building our marriage on a solid foundation that can only become stronger with You.

"Therefore, everyone who hears these words of mine and puts them into practice is like a wise man who built his house on the rock. The rain came down, the streams rose, and the winds blew and beat against that house, yet it did not fall because it had its foundation on the rock. But everyone who hears these words of mine and does not put them into practice is like a foolish man who built his house on sand. The rain came down, the streams rose, and the winds blew and beat against that house, and it fell with a great crash."

— **Matthew 7:24-27**

Jesus' parable highlights the importance of hearing and applying His teachings. The wise builder constructs his house on the rock, symbolizing the stability and security in a life grounded in obedience to God's Word. In contrast, the foolish builder's house on sand represents instability and inevitable collapse when challenges arise.

In marriage, this principle is crucial. A godly marriage built on the foundation of Christ is resilient and enduring. Storms will come—financial struggles, misunderstandings, health challenges—but a relationship rooted in God's truth will withstand them. However, if a marriage lacks this foundation, it becomes vulnerable to the pressures of life. Is your marriage currently built on the solid foundation of God's Word, or are there areas where you've been relying on unstable ground? How can you and your spouse intentionally obey God's teachings daily?

This week, set aside time to pray and study the word together. Spend five minutes daily praying as a couple, asking God for wisdom and guidance to align your marriage with His Word. Choose one passage related to love, unity, or forgiveness (e.g., 1 Corinthians 13 or Colossians 3:12-14) and discuss how it applies to your marriage. Spending time in prayer and the word together will strengthen your bond with God and each other.

Lord, thank You for being our solid foundation. Please help us to not only hear Your word but also practice it in our marriage. Strengthen us to face life's storms together, always rooted in Your truth. May our union reflect Your steadfast love and bring glory to Your name. Amen.

Week 22: Nurturing Your Bond Through Love & Communication

Heavenly Father, thank You for the gift of love that reflects Your perfect character. Teach us to embody the love described in Your word, both in our hearts and our marriages. Please help us to be patient and kind, humble and forgiving, and to seek unity and truth in all we do. Let Your love guide us in our daily interactions so we may glorify You through our love. Amen.

"Love is patient, love is kind. It does not envy, it does not boast, it is not proud. It does not dishonor others; it is not self-seeking; it is not easily angered, and it keeps no record of wrongs. Love does not delight in evil but rejoices with the truth. It always protects, always trusts, always hopes, always perseveres."

— 1 Corinthians 13:4-7

Love is an active choice, not just a feeling. It challenges us to live out love through patience, kindness, humility, forgiveness, and perseverance. In marriage, this love becomes the cornerstone of the relationship. Patience allows us to endure our spouse's imperfections with grace. Kindness reminds us to prioritize gentleness and care in our interactions. Refraining from envy or pride fosters humility and unity, while forgiveness releases us from holding onto past wrongs. Choosing to rejoice in truth and trust our spouse deepens intimacy and hope. Finally, perseverance anchors the relationship in faith, reminding us that love is steadfast even during life's trials.

When a marriage reflects this kind of love, it becomes a testimony of God's divine design, showcasing His grace and commitment to us. How can you practice patience and kindness more intentionally in your marriage? Are there any past wrongs you need to forgive or areas of pride you need to surrender to better align with God's love?

This week, practice patience and kindness. Choose one area where you've been impatient or unkind with your spouse and intentionally respond with patience and compassion instead. For example, speak softly during a moment of frustration or do an act of kindness that is significant to your spouse without being asked. There will be moments of annoyance or irritation with our spouses; we are only human, but it is important when you speak to each other to come from a kind place and speak nicely to each other as you discuss issues. Practicing kindness in all situations will take time, but the more you do it, the more it will naturally come to you. If you have a moment of showing anger towards your spouse, step back and ask for forgiveness for responding with irritation.

I also want you to identify one lingering grievance you've held onto and pray for the strength to release it. Then, share with your spouse how you choose forgiveness and invite them to join you in seeking God's healing together.

Lord, we thank You for showing us what true love looks like through Your word. Help us reflect this love in our marriage, practicing patience, kindness, forgiveness, and humility daily. Teach us to protect, trust, hope, and persevere, drawing strength from You every season. May our love bring honor to You and reflect Your unwavering commitment to us. In Jesus' name, Amen.

Week 23: Confession, Prayer, and Healing in Marriage

Heavenly Father, thank You for the gift of relationships and the opportunity to grow closer to You and each other through confession and prayer. Help us to embrace humility, grace, and honesty in our marriage, trusting in Your power to heal and restore. May our prayers reflect the righteousness You desire and bring about the healing and unity we seek. Amen.

"Therefore, confess your sins to each other and pray for each other so that you may be healed. The prayer of a righteous person is powerful and effective."

— James 5:16

James 5:16 underscores the transformative power of confession and prayer in our relationships. Confessing sins to one another creates a space for humility, accountability, and grace. It acknowledges our dependence on God's mercy and invites His healing into our lives. In the context of marriage, this verse is a powerful reminder that vulnerability and spiritual partnership strengthen the bond between husband and wife. When couples confess their shortcomings and pray for one another, they invite God's power to work in their union, fostering deeper trust, unity, and love. A marriage anchored in mutual prayer becomes a testimony to God's faithfulness and a source of spiritual healing.

Are there areas in your marriage where unspoken frustrations or unresolved conflicts hinder unity? How can confessing your struggles and praying together draw you closer as a couple and to God?

Set aside a specific time this week to confess personal struggles or shortcomings to your spouse in a safe, loving environment. Approach the conversation with humility and grace. Pray together daily for each other's needs and spiritual growth. Commit to lifting your spouse's burdens before God and seeking His guidance for your marriage.

Continually praying together and confessing our struggles to each other in marriage creates a deeper sense of unity. Phelipe and I spend time recapping our days with each other. We discuss our current struggles, from needing help around the house to extra help with the kids or challenges at work. Sharing our struggles makes us united and strengthens our bond with each other. Setting time together each week is a reminder that we are doing life together, and we need this time to build each other up to face our struggles and remain united.

Lord, thank You for the wisdom and power of Your word. Help us to apply James 5:16 to our marriage, creating an atmosphere of trust, prayer, and healing. Teach us to confess with humility, to forgive with grace, and to pray with faith. May our union reflect Your love and bring glory to Your name. Amen.

Heavenly Father, we come before You with humble hearts, seeking Your wisdom and guidance. Teach us to trust You fully in all areas of our lives, including our marriage. Help us submit to Your will and lean on Your understanding rather than our own. Bless our union with clarity, direction, and peace as we walk this journey together. In Jesus' name, Amen.

"Trust in the Lord with all your heart and lean not on your own understanding; in all your ways submit to him, and he will make your paths straight."

— Proverbs 3:5-6

This is a powerful reminder of God's faithfulness and sovereignty. It calls us to trust Him completely, even when circumstances seem uncertain or our human understanding falls short. Submitting to God means surrendering control and acknowledging that His plans are better than ours.

In marriage, this trust becomes essential. Life often brings challenges, disagreements, financial struggles, or transitions that test the foundation of a relationship. When we trust God and submit our marriage to Him, He provides wisdom, guidance, and a clear path forward. By relying on His understanding, couples can navigate difficulties with unity, knowing God directs their steps and strengthens their bond. What areas of your marriage have you been trying to control rather than trust God? How can trusting God as a couple bring peace and clarity to your relationship?

This week, identify one decision or area of tension in your marriage where you've leaned on your own understanding. Pray about it together and actively seek God's will through Scripture and reflection. Practice memorizing Psalms 115:11, which says, *"You who fear him, trust in the Lord-He is their help and shield."*

Lord, thank You for being our guide and protector. Help us to trust You more each day and to surrender our marriage to Your will. Teach us to walk in unity, seeking Your wisdom in every decision. Strengthen our love for one another as we lean on Your understanding, not our own. Lead us on the path You have prepared for us, and may our marriage glorify You in all we do. Amen.

Week 25: Strength in Faith and Courage in Marriage

Heavenly Father, thank You for the gift of Your Word, which strengthens and equips us to face life's challenges. As we reflect on this scripture today, help us to stand firm in our faith, be courageous, and grow stronger in our commitment to You and each other. Teach us how to live out these truths in our marriage so that we may glorify You. Amen.

"Wait for the Lord; be strong and take heart and wait for the Lord."

— Psalms 27:14

This verse reminds us that waiting on the Lord is not passive but an act of trust and faith. The psalmist encourages us to be strong and courageous, knowing that God's timing is perfect, even when we don't see the whole picture. Waiting for the Lord involves surrendering control, leaning on His strength, and trusting that He works all things together for good.

This principle is compelling in marriage. Couples often face uncertainties—whether about finances, parenting, career transitions, or health struggles. Waiting on the Lord together strengthens the bond between spouses as they learn to rely not only on each other but also on God's wisdom and timing. It's an opportunity to grow in patience, resilience, and unity, knowing that God's plans are always better than our own.

This week, identify a "Waiting" area. Choose one aspect of your life where you feel called to wait on the Lord. Write down a Bible verse about trust or patience and display it where you and your spouse can see it daily as a reminder.

Lord, we thank You for the reminder that Your plans are greater than ours and that You are with us as we wait. Help us grow stronger in faith and courage, trusting Your timing in every aspect of our lives and marriage. May our unity reflect Your love and glorify You through our patience and trust. In Jesus' name, Amen.

Week 26: Love and Respect in Marriage

Thank You for the gift of marriage and the guidance You provide through Your word. Teach us to love and respect one another as You have called us to, reflecting the beauty of Your love in our relationship. Help us honor this sacred bond and seek Your wisdom daily in caring for each other. Amen.

"However, each one of you also must love his wife as he loves himself, and the wife must respect her husband."

— Ephesians 5:33

This verse encapsulates the essence of a Godly marriage: love and respect. Husbands are called to love their wives with the same selfless, sacrificial love Christ shows for His church. This means prioritizing their wife's well-being, cherishing her, and making her feel secure in his love. In turn, wives are encouraged to respect their husbands, recognize their leadership, support them, and affirm their role in the partnership. It highlights the complementary needs of love and respect. While every person values both, many husbands thrive on respect and wives on love. When these needs are met, a harmonious and God-centered marriage is cultivated. This mutual devotion mirrors the relationship between Christ and His church, serving as a living testimony of God's grace and unity.

How can you better demonstrate love or respect in your marriage this week? How does understanding your spouse's unique needs for love or respect strengthen your relationship? This week, I challenge you as a couple. Husbands: show intentional acts of love this week. This could mean planning a thoughtful date night, offering encouragement, or helping with a task your wife values. Wives: express genuine respect for your husband. Acknowledge his efforts, speak kindly about him, and show appreciation for his role in your life.

Lord, thank You for Your perfect design for marriage. Help us to love and respect each other as You have commanded, reflecting Your love in our daily actions and words. Strengthen our bond and guide us to build a marriage that honors You and brings glory to Your name. May our union be a witness of Your grace and faithfulness to those around us. In Jesus' name, we pray. Amen.

Week 27: Strengthening Physical Intimacy

Heavenly Father, thank You for the gift of marriage and the intimacy that strengthens our bond as husband and wife. Help us to honor You in our relationship and to prioritize both spiritual devotion and our unity as a couple. Open our hearts to understand Your word and guide us in applying it to our marriage. Amen.

"Do not deprive each other except perhaps by mutual consent and for a time so that you may devote yourselves to prayer. Then come together again so that Satan will not tempt you because of your lack of self-control."

— 1 Corinthians 7:5

Paul addresses the importance of physical and spiritual intimacy within the marital relationship. He acknowledges that there may be times when a couple agrees to abstain from physical intimacy for spiritual purposes, such as prayer and fasting. However, he advises that this should only be temporary and mutually agreed upon to prevent temptation or discord.

In marriage, physical intimacy is not just a physical act; it is a gift from God designed to strengthen the bond between husband and wife. Paul highlights that the connection in marriage mirrors our spiritual relationship with God, built on mutual respect, trust, and shared devotion. By aligning your physical and spiritual lives, you safeguard your marriage against external pressures and temptations.

Are there areas in your marriage where you could better balance spiritual devotion and physical intimacy? How can you

157

and your spouse work together to strengthen your spiritual connection with God and each other? Schedule a specific time to pray as a couple this week. Pray for your needs and marriage, seeking God's guidance in nurturing intimacy and unity.

Have an open conversation. Discuss with your spouse how to align spiritual and physical intimacy in your relationship. Be honest and intentional about ways to support each other's physical needs.

Lord, we thank You for the wisdom of Your word and the sacred bond of marriage. Please help us find harmony in our relationship, honoring our union's spiritual and physical aspects. Give us the strength to guard our marriage against temptation and grow closer to You and one another. May Your grace guide us in love, respect, and unity. Amen.

Week 28: Mutual Love and Submission in Marriage

Heavenly Father, we thank You for the gift of marriage, a sacred union You designed to reflect your love and faithfulness. Help us to embrace the spirit of selflessness as we seek to honor You and each other in our relationship. Open our hearts and minds to understand and apply Your word in our marriage. In Jesus' name, we pray. Amen.

"The wife does not have authority over her own body but yields it to her husband. In the same way, the husband does not have authority over his own body but yields it to his wife."

— 1 Corinthians 7:4

This verse emphasizes mutual submission and selflessness in marriage. It reflects a sacred truth: marriage is a partnership built on love, respect, and unity. Neither spouse is independent of the other; instead, they belong to one another in a way that mirrors Christ's love for the Church—a sacrificial, giving, and deeply relational love.

In marriage, yielding to one another is not about dominance or control but about offering yourself in love, trust, and service. This mutual giving honors God's design for marriage, where both spouses are equally valued and committed to each other's well-being. It calls for vulnerability and trust, reminding us that marriage is a safe space to love and be loved without reservation.

It challenges us to set aside selfishness and instead embrace a Christ-like posture of putting our spouse's needs above our own. It's about creating a bond that thrives on mutual respect, care, and dedication to each other's growth and happiness.

In what areas of your marriage can you show more selflessness and care for your spouse's needs?

How can mutual submission strengthen the trust and intimacy in your relationship? For this week, show intentional selflessness. Identify one specific way to meet your spouse's needs this week—whether through an act of service, quality time, or emotional support—and follow through with it.

Lord, thank You for the gift of marriage and Your word, which guides us in loving each other well. Teach us to live out the principles of mutual submission and selflessness, just as You love us unconditionally. Strengthen our bond and help us to honor You through our marriage. May our union reflect Your grace, love, and faithfulness. In Jesus' name, we pray. Amen.

Week 29: Forgive as the Lord Forgave You

Heavenly Father, thank You for the gift of forgiveness that You have freely given through Your Son, Jesus Christ. Help me to embrace a heart of compassion and grace in my marriage, reflecting Your love through patience and forgiveness. Open my heart to release grievances and build a stronger unity with my spouse, all for Your glory. Amen.

"Bear with each other and forgive one another if any of you has a grievance against someone. Forgive as the Lord forgave you."

— Colossians 3:13

Paul calls us to imitate Christ's forgiveness in our relationships. Forgiveness is not conditional or optional but a command to reflect the grace we've received from God. In marriage, where emotions run deep and imperfections often surface, grievances can build walls between spouses. However, God's example of forgiveness challenges us to dismantle those barriers by offering grace to one another.

Forgiveness in marriage is about choosing reconciliation over resentment. Just as God doesn't hold our sins against us but washes them away thoroughly, we are called to release the offenses of our spouse. This doesn't mean ignoring pain or justifying wrongs but recognizing that forgiveness frees both the giver and receiver, fostering healing and unity in the relationship. Is there an unresolved grievance I am holding onto in my marriage that needs forgiveness? How can I better model God's forgiveness when conflicts arise with my spouse? This week, pray daily for forgiveness. Set aside time each day to ask God to help you forgive your spouse or anyone you may be holding a grievance against. Pray specifically for areas of tension and ask for His peace to cover your heart.

Express forgiveness tangibly: Take one concrete action this week to show your spouse grace. This could be through a kind note, an unexpected act of service, or a heartfelt conversation to reconcile any lingering disagreements.

Lord, I thank You for showing me what true forgiveness looks like. Teach me to forgive my spouse as You have forgiven me, with a heart full of love and compassion. Strengthen our marriage by helping us release and replace grievances with understanding and grace. Let our relationship reflect Your mercy, and may we grow closer to each other as we draw closer to You. Amen.

Week 30: Trusting God's Promises Together

Father, thank You for Your faithfulness and unwavering promises. As we reflect on Your word, open our hearts to see the beauty of trusting in Your plan, even when the circumstances seem impossible. Teach us to rely on You as Sarah did, to walk by faith, and to honor Your promises in every area of our lives, especially in our marriages. In Jesus' name, we pray. Amen.

"And by faith, even Sarah, who was past childbearing age, was enabled to bear children because she considered him faithful who had made the promise."

— Hebrews 11:11

This verse highlights the power of faith in God's promises. Sarah faced the impossible situation of bearing a child when she was well beyond childbearing age. Yet, by trusting in God's faithfulness, she saw His promise fulfilled. It wasn't Sarah's circumstances or strength that brought the promise to pass, but her belief in the One who made the promise.

We often encounter insurmountable financial struggles, communication barriers, or emotional distance in marriage. Like Sarah, we're called to believe in God's ability to work through these difficulties. Trusting in God's promises enables us to persevere, grow closer, and see His blessings unfold in our union.

God's faithfulness depends not on our strength but on His unchanging nature. As couples, when we believe in His promises and align our marriage with His will, we witness the

163

miraculous, even in life's everyday challenges. This week, recall God's faithfulness. Write down three moments in your relationship where you've seen God's promises fulfilled or His faithfulness in action. Share them with your spouse and thank God for His work in your lives.

Thank You for being a God who keeps His promises. Help us to walk by faith as Sarah did, trusting in Your perfect plan for our marriage. Strengthen our bond as we lean on You, and teach us to see Your faithfulness in every relationship season. May our marriage be a reflection of Your love and steadfastness. In Jesus' name, Amen.

Week 31: Loyalty in Marriage

Heavenly Father, thank You for the example of faithfulness and devotion seen in the story of Ruth and Boaz. Help us to love and serve selflessly, reflecting Your grace in our relationships. Open our hearts to learn from Your word today, and guide us in applying these lessons to our marriages. In Jesus' name, we pray. Amen.

"Boaz replied, 'I've been told all about what you have done for your mother-in-law since the death of your husband—how you left your father and mother and your homeland and came to live with a people you did not know before."

— Ruth 2:11

This highlights Ruth's unwavering commitment to Naomi, her mother-in-law, despite the challenges she faced. Ruth's loyalty, sacrifice, and willingness to leave behind her comfort zone reveal her deep character and trust in God's plan. Boaz, noticing these qualities, acknowledges Ruth's faithfulness and is drawn to her integrity.

In marriage, this passage serves as a reminder of the sacrifices and commitments required to build a strong, God-centered relationship. Just as Ruth chose to love and serve despite hardship, marriage calls for selfless devotion, leaving behind personal preferences or familiar ways for the sake of unity and partnership. When we prioritize faithfulness and love, God blesses the work of our hands and hearts, as seen in the eventual union of Ruth and Boaz. How can Ruth's faithfulness inspire you to show selfless love and commitment in your marriage? Are there areas in your relationship where you need to trust God more fully, as Ruth did when stepping into the unknown?

This week, I served selflessly. Identify one way to serve your spouse this week without expecting anything in return. This could be taking over a chore they dislike or surprising them with something meaningful. I also want you to plan an activity that stretches you as a couple, such as volunteering, tackling a new project, or even having an honest conversation about future goals and challenges while trusting God's guidance.

Lord, thank You for Ruth's example of steadfast love and courage. Please help us to reflect on these qualities in our marriage. Teach us to serve each other with humility and grace, even when facing challenges. May we trust in Your plans and lean on Your guidance to grow closer as a couple. Bless our efforts this week to honor You in our relationship. Amen.

Week 32: A Marriage of Service and Sacrifice

Heavenly Father, thank You for the example of Priscilla and Aquila, a couple devoted to serving You and supporting others in faith. Help us to embody their courage, unity, and love in our marriage. Teach us to serve each other selflessly and others, glorifying You in all we do. Amen.

"Greet Priscilla and Aquila, my coworkers in Christ Jesus. They risked their lives for me. Not only I but all the churches of the Gentiles are grateful to them. Greet also the church that meets at their house."

— Romans 16:3-5

Paul honors Priscilla and Aquila, a married couple who worked tirelessly to support his ministry and the early church. Their lives reflect a deep commitment to God and a shared purpose in advancing His kingdom. They modeled a partnership rooted in faith, service, and sacrifice by risking their lives for Paul and hosting a church in their home.

This scripture reminds us that marriage is about companionship and mutual devotion to God's work. A Godly marriage creates a strong foundation for serving together, encouraging one another in faith, and impacting others through hospitality, courage, and love. How does your marriage reflect a partnership in serving God and others? How can you and your spouse grow in courage and sacrifice as Priscilla and Aquila did? This week, identify one act of service you can do as a couple, whether volunteering at church, hosting a small group, or helping a friend in need.

Lord, thank You for the beautiful example of Priscilla and Aquila, who served You together with courage and love. Help us build a marriage reflecting their faithfulness and commitment to Your mission. May our lives and homes be places of light and service, pointing others to Your grace. Strengthen our bond as we work together for Your glory. Amen.

Heavenly Father, thank You for the wisdom You provide through Your Word. Teach us to listen with open hearts, to speak with grace, and to control our emotions with patience. Help us grow in love and understanding within our marriage, reflecting Your character in our actions and words. In Jesus' name, we pray. Amen.

"My dear brothers and sisters, take note of this: Everyone should be quick to listen, slow to speak, and slow to become angry."

— James 1:19

James 1:19 offers timeless guidance for fostering peace and harmony in relationships, particularly in marriage. The verse emphasizes the importance of listening attentively, choosing words wisely, and maintaining calm. In the context of marriage, this wisdom helps us avoid misunderstandings, defuse conflicts, and build a foundation of mutual respect and trust.

When we are "quick to listen," we demonstrate care and empathy, prioritizing our spouse's feelings and perspective. Being "slow to speak" reminds us to think before responding, ensuring our words build up rather than tear down. Finally, being "slow to become angry" reflects the grace and patience God shows us, allowing space for love to thrive even during disagreements. How can you become a better listener to your spouse this week? How do you typically respond in moments of frustration, and how can I align my reactions with God's teaching in this verse?

This week, practice intentional listening. Set aside time this week to listen to your spouse without interrupting or formulating a response. Focus on understanding their perspective fully and pause before responding. Commit to a "three-second rule" before speaking during challenging conversations. This pause can help you respond with thoughtfulness and grace rather than reacting impulsively.

Thank You for Your word, which equips us to love as You love. Please help us to be quick to listen, slow to speak, and slow to anger in our marriage. Give us the humility to put each other's needs before our own, the patience to grow together, and the wisdom to resolve conflicts with love. May our words and actions reflect Your grace and bring glory to You. Amen.

Heavenly Father, we come before You, grateful for the love You have poured into our lives. Help us reflect Your divine love in our marriage and relationships. Teach us to love one another with patience, kindness, and a selfless heart. May Your Spirit guide us in becoming more like You, the perfect source of love. Amen.

"Beloved, let us love one another, for love is of God; and everyone who loves is born of God and knows God."

— 1 John 4:7

Love originates from God. We truly understand what it means to love through knowing Him. In marriage, this divine love becomes the foundation of unity. Spouses should view themselves as one that will cultivate a successful marriage because both of you will put in all your efforts to work, serve, and give whatever it takes to build a great union. God calls us to mirror His unconditional, patient, and sacrificial love in our relationship with our spouse.

When we love as God loves, we live out His will and demonstrate His presence in our marriage. This means setting aside selfish desires, listening with empathy, and forgiving without keeping a record of wrongs. As we embody God's love, our marriage is a testimony to His transformative power.

How can you show more of God's unconditional love to your spouse, even during conflict or frustration? In what ways does your love reflect your relationship with God? This week, practice daily acts of love towards your spouse. Each day, find one specific way to show love to your spouse that reflects God's love, whether through a kind word, a selfless act, or simply listening intently.

Father, thank You for showing us the perfect example of love through Your Son, Jesus. Help us draw closer to You so that we can reflect Your love in our marriage. Teach us to love selflessly and strengthen our bond through acts of kindness, patience, and understanding. May Your love be the foundation upon which we build our lives together. In Jesus' name, Amen.

Heavenly Father, thank You for calling us to live a life of righteousness and peace. Help us as a couple to turn away from temptations and pursue faith, love, and unity in our marriage. Let our hearts remain pure before You, and may we honor You in our thoughts, words, and actions. Amen.

"Flee the evil desires of youth and pursue righteousness, faith, love, and peace, along with those who call on the Lord out of a pure heart."

— 2 Timothy 2:22

God calls us to turn away from youthful temptations—those selfish or impulsive desires that can damage relationships—and instead chase after qualities that strengthen our relationship with God and others: righteousness, faith, love, and peace. In marriage, these principles are foundational. Pursuing righteousness means living in alignment with God's will, prioritizing integrity and selflessness. Faith binds you together as you trust God in all circumstances, while love and peace create an environment where understanding and forgiveness can flourish.

This verse also emphasizes the importance of surrounding yourself with others who share a sincere commitment to God. Marriage includes encouraging each other to seek God's presence and making Him the cornerstone of your relationship. When you intentionally flee temptations and strive for God-honoring virtues, you build a marriage that reflects His design and glorifies Him.

Are there specific desires, habits, or distractions you need to flee as a couple to honor God more fully in your marriage? How can you encourage others to pursue righteousness, faith, love, and peace daily?

This week, set boundaries together by identifying one or two areas where temptation or distractions might creep into your marriage (e.g., media, negative communication, or time mismanagement). Create practical boundaries to guard your relationship. Pursue a shared devotional practice. Spend time together each day in prayer or reading scripture, focusing on God's attributes. Discuss how you can apply these traits in your marriage.

Lord, we commit to fleeing the desires that can pull us away from You and each other. Help us to grow in righteousness, faith, love, and peace as we pursue Your will for our marriage. May our hearts remain pure, and may our union reflect Your grace and love to those around us. In Jesus' name, Amen.

Week 36: Restoring Harmony in Marriage

Thank You for Your Word, which guides us in loving, forgiving, and communicating with one another. Please help us to approach our spouse with humility and grace when conflict arises. Teach us to restore relationships with love and wisdom, just as You have restored us through Christ. Amen.

"If your brother or sister sins, go and point out their fault, just between the two of you. If they listen to you, you have won them over."

— Matthew 18:15

This verse from Matthew is a call to practice reconciliation in relationships through private, respectful, and loving confrontation. While it primarily addresses conflicts among believers, its principles are highly relevant to marriage. Conflicts are inevitable within the sacred union of marriage, but how we handle them can strengthen or weaken the bond we share with our spouse.

It emphasizes addressing issues directly, without gossip or public criticism. Issues should be discussed privately between you and your spouse. They should not be discussed publicly with other family members or friends. This means approaching your spouse lovingly and focusing on resolving the issue rather than assigning blame. When done with humility and a desire for restoration, such conversations can deepen trust and strengthen the marital bond.

How do you typically handle conflict in your marriage? Do you seek to resolve it privately and lovingly, or let it fester? What steps can you take to ensure that your approach to confrontation reflects love and respect for your spouse? This week, plan a private conversation. If there is an unresolved issue with your spouse, set aside a quiet time this week to discuss it calmly and respectfully. Focus on the issue, not the person, and seek mutual understanding.

Lord, thank You for showing us the path to reconciliation and peace. Help us to approach our spouse with humility, patience, and love when addressing conflicts. Teach us to speak truth in love, listen with understanding, and forgive as You forgive us. May our marriage reflect Your grace and bring You glory. In Jesus' name, Amen.

Week 37: Pursuing Peace in Marriage

Heavenly Father, we come before You with hearts open to Your wisdom. Teach us to seek peace in our relationships and guide us to reflect your love and grace in our marriage. Please help us to choose unity over discord and forgiveness over resentment. May Your Spirit lead us to live in harmony, as You intended. In Jesus' name, Amen.

"If it is possible, as far as it depends on you, live at peace with everyone."

— Romans 12:18

This emphasizes the importance of personal responsibility in fostering peace. While conflict is inevitable in life, including marriage, God calls us to do everything we can to maintain harmony. Living at peace doesn't mean avoiding hard conversations or compromising truth but prioritizing understanding, humility, and love. In marriage, this principle teaches us to approach disagreements with grace, seeking solutions instead of placing blame and remembering that a peaceful marriage glorifies God.

Peace in marriage requires intentional effort and selflessness. It involves controlling our words, showing patience, and forgiving offenses. By focusing on what we can do rather than what we expect from our spouse, we can create an atmosphere of trust and love where peace can thrive. There is a quote by author Melissa Spino that says, "The only person you can control is yourself. You alone can choose how you

177

feel, your attitude, your behavior, your response." You only have control over yourself, so choose today to foster peace in your marriage.

Are there unresolved conflicts in your marriage where you could take steps toward reconciliation? How can you demonstrate humility and grace during moments of disagreement with your spouse? This week, practice daily acts of kindness. Choose one way each day to show your spouse love and appreciation, whether through words, actions, or small surprises. These gestures reinforce unity and foster peace.

Lord, thank You for Your Word guiding us in our relationships. Help us to live out this verse in our marriage, pursuing peace and reflecting Your love. Give us wisdom to navigate conflicts with grace and hearts that are quick to forgive. May our marriage be a testimony of Your goodness and Your peace. Amen.

Heavenly Father, thank You for the gift of marriage and the opportunity to grow in love and unity with our spouse. Teach us to reflect Your grace in how we forgive, just as You have graciously forgiven us. Soften our hearts and guide us in making room for each other's imperfections. Help us cultivate a marriage rooted in compassion, humility, and love. Amen.

"Make allowance for each other's faults, and forgive anyone who offends you. Remember, the Lord forgave you, so you must forgive others."

— Colossians 3:13

Forgiveness is central to a Christ-centered marriage. Colossians 3:13 reminds us that just as God forgives us for our sins, we are called to extend that same grace to others, especially our spouse. In marriage, both partners are imperfect, and offenses—whether small or significant—are inevitable. Forgiveness is not about condoning hurtful actions but freeing ourselves and our spouse from resentment. It creates space for healing, growth, and deeper connection.

Forgiveness in marriage also means making allowances for each other's faults and understanding that we all have weaknesses. It's about choosing love over irritation and grace over anger, modeling Christ's sacrificial love. When we forgive, we reflect God's character and build a relationship founded on mutual respect and compassion.

Are there any unresolved hurts or offenses in your marriage that you must bring before God and address with your spouse? How can embracing God's forgiveness in your own life help you extend that grace to your spouse?

Commit to daily prayer for forgiveness. Each day this week, pray and ask God to help you release any lingering resentment or bitterness in your heart. Pray specifically for areas where you need to forgive or seek forgiveness from your spouse. Practice grace in real time. When your spouse makes a mistake, pause before reacting. Choose to respond with understanding, making an intentional effort to "make allowance" for their faults.

Lord, thank You for the gift of forgiveness and for showing us what grace truly looks like through Jesus. Help us to mirror Your forgiveness in our marriage. Teach us to let go of offenses and to approach each other with compassion and understanding. May our marriage reflect Your love and forgiveness, bringing glory to Your name. Amen.

Lord, thank You for the gift of marriage and the sacred bond between husband and wife. Help us to love and serve each other selflessly, fulfilling the roles You have designed for us. Teach us to honor You in our marriage by embracing the duties we owe to one another with joy and devotion. May our relationship reflect Your unconditional love and grace. Amen.

"The husband should fulfill his marital duty to his wife, and likewise the wife to her husband."

—1 Corinthians 7:3

It is the mutual responsibility of spouses to meet each other's needs in marriage, whether emotional, physical, or spiritual. The "marital duty" Paul refers to isn't merely about physical intimacy but encompasses every aspect of love, care, and commitment. Marriage is a covenant where both partners are called to serve one another selflessly, just as Christ loves and serves His Church.

In marriage, fulfilling our duties is not about obligation or scorekeeping—it is about giving from a place of love and reverence for God. When both spouses prioritize each other's needs, the relationship grows in trust, unity, and strength. This principle helps to create a balanced partnership where love is nurtured and God is glorified.

How have you intentionally met your spouse's emotional, physical, or spiritual needs? How can you ensure your acts of love and service stem from selflessness rather than obligation? This week, communicate needs openly. This week, have an honest conversation with your spouse about how you can better meet each other's needs. Create a safe space for open dialogue without judgment.

Lord, thank You for the beautiful gift of marriage and the opportunity to reflect Your love through our relationship. Please help us serve each other joyfully and humbly, always putting our needs above ours. May our marriage be a testimony of Your grace and faithfulness to the world. Teach us to grow in unity and love, keeping You at the center of all we do. In Jesus' name, we pray. Amen.

Week 40: Honoring Each Other in Marriage

Lord, thank You for the gift of marriage and the opportunity to honor and serve one another as You have called us. Please help us to surrender our selfish desires and embrace your design for unity in our relationship. May we reflect Your love and grace in the way we care for each other. Guide us today as we reflect on Your word and teach us to live out this truth in our marriage. Amen.

"The wife does not have authority over her own body but yields it to her husband. In the same way, the husband does not have authority over his own body but yields it to his wife."

— 1 Corinthians 7:4

Marriage entails mutual selflessness and deep unity. In a Godly marriage, both husband and wife must lay aside their individual needs and prioritize one another's needs, desires, and well-being. This surrender is not about control but sacrificial love, which is giving freely and honoring the covenant made before God. It reflects Christ's sacrificial love for the Church, where each partner seeks to serve and build the other up in love and respect.

This verse challenges us to reject selfishness in marriage and instead embrace a mindset of mutual care and dedication. It speaks to the emotional, physical, and spiritual intimacy that strengthens the bond between husband and wife. When both partners commit to honoring and serving one another, they experience a more profound connection rooted in God's love and design for unity.

In what areas of your marriage could you practice selflessness and prioritize your spouse's needs over your own? How does yielding to your spouse, as described in this verse, reflect Christ's sacrificial love for us? Serve your spouse this week by planning a special moment to show appreciation.

Lord, thank You for the wisdom and guidance You provide in Your Word. Help us to embody the selfless love You have shown us in our marriage. Teach us to honor and serve one another with humility and grace, reflecting Your perfect love. Strengthen our bond as we seek to put You at the center of our relationship. May we grow in unity and trust, constantly surrendering to Your will. In Jesus' name, we pray. Amen.

Father, thank You for the gift of marriage and the opportunity to reflect Your love and goodness within our union. Teach us to value noble character in ourselves and our spouse. Help us bless each other, bringing joy, trust, and honor into our marriage. Guide us as we grow in faith, love, and partnership, building a relationship that glorifies You. Amen.

"A wife of noble character who can find? She is worth far more than rubies. Her husband has full confidence in her and lacks nothing of value. She brings him good, not harm, all the days of her life."

— Proverbs 31:10-12

This passage from Proverbs 31 celebrates the virtues of a godly wife. Her noble character, rooted in integrity, wisdom, and love, is portrayed as a priceless treasure. This character instills confidence in her husband, building trust and mutual respect in their marriage. She actively contributes to the well-being of her household, choosing to be a source of encouragement and support.

In marriage, this verse reminds both partners of their calling to prioritize virtues that honor God and strengthen their union. It challenges wives to embody grace and wisdom and encourages husbands to cherish and trust their wives as valuable partners. Together, these qualities form a foundation of love and respect, creating a marriage that reflects God's design.

This week, consider cultivating a noble character as a spouse to strengthen your marriage. Please write a note or share verbally with your spouse specific qualities you admire about them and how they bring goodness.

Thank You for the wisdom and encouragement found in Your word. Please help us to embody the qualities of noble character in our marriage. Teach us to cherish and honor one another, building trust and joy in our relationship. May we reflect Your love through our actions, words, and choices, bringing glory to You in all we do. In Jesus' name, we pray. Amen.

Week 42: The Unyielding Power of Love

Lord, thank You for the gift of love that reflects Your unending and sacrificial love for us. As we reflect on Your Word today, open our hearts to understand the depth, strength, and beauty of the love You desire in our lives and marriages. Teach us to love with a devotion that reflects Your covenant, and guide us to keep our commitment to one another strong and unshaken. In Jesus' name, Amen.

"Place me like a seal over your heart, like a seal on your arm, for love is as strong as death, its jealousy unyielding as the grave. It burns like blazing fire, like a mighty flame. Many waters cannot quench love; rivers cannot sweep it away. If one were to give all the wealth of one's house for love, it would be utterly scorned."

— Song of Solomon 8:6-7

This verse poetically captures true love's power, permanence, and pricelessness. The imagery of a "seal" over the heart and arm symbolizes unbreakable commitment and public declaration. In its purest form, love is compared to death and fire—inescapable and all-consuming. Its intensity is beyond human wealth and power, a gift of divine origin that external challenges cannot extinguish.

In marriage, this verse reminds us of the covenantal nature of love, a bond that mirrors God's steadfast love for His people. True marital love is unwavering and enduring, surviving life's challenges. It is not transactional or conditional but sacrificial and deeply rooted in trust, passion, and devotion. This kind of love can only flourish when God is at its center, fueling and protecting it through His grace.

How does the imagery of a "seal" over the heart and arm challenge you to think about the level of commitment in your marriage? What steps can you take to ensure that the love in your marriage is unquenchable, even amid life's challenges? This week, write a heartfelt letter to your spouse expressing your commitment to them, reflecting on the qualities that make your love strong and unique.

Father God, thank You for showing us what perfect love looks like through Your word and the sacrifice of Jesus. Help us protect and cherish our marriage's love as a reflection of Your unyielding love for us. Guide us to build a foundation of trust, commitment, and grace that nothing can shake. May our love burn brightly, enduring all trials and glorifying You in all we do. Amen.

Week 43: Cultivating Humility and Understanding

Father, we come before You with hearts ready to learn and grow in humility. Teach us to love as You love, valuing one another above ourselves. Help us to reflect Your selfless grace in our marriage, seeking to serve and honor each other daily. May Your word shape our hearts and transform our relationship. Amen.

"Do nothing out of selfish ambition or vain conceit. Rather, in humility, value others above yourselves, not looking to your own interests but each of you to the interests of the others."

— Philippians 2:3-4

This passage from Philippians calls us to a Christlike mindset, emphasizing humility, selflessness, and love. Paul encourages believers to set aside pride and selfish ambition, prioritizing the needs and well-being of others above their own.

In the context of marriage, these verses remind us that our union is not about seeking personal gain or being "right" but about mutual sacrifice and serving one another. A marriage rooted in humility mirrors Christ's love for the church—selfless, sacrificial, and honoring. When we consider our spouse's needs, desires, and perspectives, we build a relationship that reflects God's grace.

In what ways can you practice humility in your marriage this week? Identify one specific way to meet a need or bring joy to your spouse this week without expecting anything in return. This could be taking on a household task they dislike or planning a surprise act of kindness.

Lord, we thank You for the gift of marriage and the opportunity to grow together in humility and love. Teach us to value each other as You value us, putting aside our pride and selfish desires. Help us to honor one another in our words, actions, and thoughts, reflecting Your grace in our relationship. Guide us as we seek to build a marriage that glorifies You. In Jesus' name, we pray. Amen.

Week 44: Embracing Challenges as a Path to Hope in Marriage

Heavenly Father, we come before You with grateful hearts, knowing You are with us in every season of life. Teach us to embrace challenges with faith and perseverance, trusting that You are working in and through our trials to strengthen our relationship with You and each other. Fill our hearts with Your love through the Holy Spirit as we reflect on Your word today. Amen.

"Not only so, but we also glory in our sufferings because we know that suffering produces perseverance; perseverance, character; and character, hope. And hope does not put us to shame because God's love has been poured out into our hearts through the Holy Spirit, who has been given to us."

— Romans 5:3-5

This passage reminds us that struggles are not without purpose. In the context of marriage, challenges often feel overwhelming—financial strains, miscommunication, or differing priorities can shake the foundation of our union. Yet, God calls us to "glory in our sufferings," not because we enjoy pain but because we know He is using it to shape us.

Challenges in marriage can refine us as individuals and as a couple, teaching perseverance to face hardships together. This perseverance builds character, revealing the strength of God's presence in our lives. From this character springs hope. I hope God's plan for your marriage is far greater than you can imagine. The Holy Spirit empowers us with God's love, enabling us to endure trials and emerge stronger together.

191

Marriage is a divine reflection of God's love for His people, but it also works and requires our time and commitment to make it last. Thankfully, we can have a successful and fulfilling marriage with God's help and his words about marriage.

How can you view your marital struggles as opportunities to grow in perseverance and character together? What areas of your relationship must be entrusted to God for healing and renewal? Set aside time to pray for your marriage each day, asking God to strengthen your bond and guide you through challenges with hope.

Loving Father, thank You for the promise that our trials are not in vain. Help us see our struggles as opportunities to grow closer to You and one another. May Your Holy Spirit fill our hearts with love, patience, and hope as we navigate the challenges in our marriage. Strengthen us to persevere, shape our character, and fill us with the hope that we will never disappoint. We trust You to guide us and keep our hearts united in Your love. In Jesus' name, Amen.

Week 45: Strength in Unity

Heavenly Father, thank You for the gift of partnership and the reminder that we are stronger together. Please help us to honor and support one another in all we do, lifting each other when we stumble and celebrating each other's victories. Guide our hearts to embrace the unity You have designed for us so that our relationship reflects Your love and wisdom. Amen.

"Two are better than one because they have a good return for their labor: If either of them falls down, one can help the other up."

— Ecclesiastes 4:9-10

This passage reminds us of the power of partnership, particularly within marriage. It highlights the strength and purpose of two people working together toward shared goals. In marriage, this means sharing responsibilities, providing emotional and spiritual support, and being a source of encouragement during tough times.

The verse also speaks to the importance of being present for one another. When one spouse falters—whether in faith, health, or life's challenges—the other can step in with love and strength. This mutual care mirrors God's relationship design: to be rooted in love, unity, and selflessness.

This truth is a call to action. It reminds us that together, we are better equipped to handle life's burdens and celebrate its blessings. By leaning on each other and trusting God as the foundation of the relationship, couples can face any challenge with resilience and grace. In what ways have you and your spouse lifted each other during difficult times? This week, we will work on a shared task together. Choose a task or project you've been meaning to tackle—whether it's a chore, budgeting, or planning a future event—and complete it as a team. Use this as an opportunity to build unity and trust.

Lord, thank You for blessing the marriage partnership. Help us to support each other as You have called us to, lifting one another with love and grace. Teach us to rely on Your wisdom and work together in unity, knowing that our bond is strengthened through You. May our marriage reflect Your goodness and be a testimony of Your faithfulness. In Jesus' name, Amen.

Week 46: Sharing and Carrying Each Other's Burdens

Heavenly Father, we come before You with grateful hearts, asking for Your guidance in our marriage. Teach us to carry each other's burdens with love and compassion, just as Christ carries ours. Please help us to be a source of strength and encouragement for one another as we walk this journey together. May your word shape our actions and bring us closer as a couple. Amen.

"Carry each other's burdens, and in this way, you will fulfill the law of Christ."

— Galatians 6:2

This speaks to the heart of Christian love and service. Carrying one another's burdens means stepping into each other's struggles with compassion and humility. It reflects Christ's sacrificial love, who bore our most significant burden—sin—on the cross. In marriage, this principle is of profound importance. Partners are called to share life's weight, whether it be emotional struggles, physical challenges, or spiritual battles. By shouldering each other's burdens, you embody Christ's love and fulfill His law, which is rooted in love for God and others.

This verse reminds us that marriage is not a solo journey but a partnership designed to support, uplift, and grow together in unity. Are there specific burdens your spouse carries right now that you can help lighten? Take intentional

195

action to help lighten that burden this week. This could mean praying with them daily, taking over a task they find stressful, or simply offering words of affirmation and understanding.

Lord, thank You for the gift of marriage and the opportunity to reflect Your love by carrying each other's burdens. Help us to see our spouse's needs with Your eyes and respond with a willing heart. Strengthen us as a couple to live out Your law of love, making our relationship a testament to Your grace. May we glorify You in our actions and grow closer to one another as we trust in You. Amen.

Week 47: Living in Peace in Marriage

Heavenly Father, thank You for the gift of peace and the call to pursue harmony in our relationships. Help us to live in a way that reflects Your love and grace, especially in our marriage. Open our hearts to understand Your word today, and guide us in applying it in ways that strengthen our bond. Amen.

"If it is possible, as far as it depends on you, live at peace with everyone."

— Romans 12:18

It is our responsibility to seek peace in all relationships, including marriage. While we cannot control the actions of others, we are called to do our part in fostering harmony. In marriage, this means taking the initiative to resolve conflicts, showing grace, and being willing to listen and understand. Living in peace doesn't mean avoiding hard conversations; it means addressing issues with humility, patience, and a desire for reconciliation.

Marriage is a covenant where both partners commit to reflecting Christ's love. This requires effort, sacrifice, and intentionality to create an environment of peace. By relying on God's wisdom and grace, we can overcome misunderstandings and build a relationship that honors Him. Are there areas in your marriage where peace has been disrupted? What steps can you take to address them? Each day this week, thank your spouse for one specific thing they did or said. This practice fosters a spirit of appreciation and softens hearts. I also want you to identify one unresolved issue in your marriage. Set aside time to discuss it calmly, focusing on understanding rather than winning the argument. Pray together before the conversation for wisdom and unity.

Lord, thank You for Your peace that surpasses all understanding. Help us to reflect Your grace in our marriage, striving to live in harmony even during challenging moments. Teach us to love one another as You love us, showing patience, forgiveness, and understanding. Let our marriage be a testimony of Your peace and a light to those around us. In Jesus' name, Amen.

Week 48: Honoring God in Marriage Through Respect

Heavenly Father, we come to You today seeking wisdom and understanding as we dive into Your word. Teach us to show respect to everyone, love deeply, and honor You in every part of our lives, especially in our marriages. Please help us reflect on Your grace and humility when treating one another. In Jesus' name, we pray. Amen.

"Show proper respect to everyone, love the family of believers, fear God, honor the emperor."

— 1 Peter 2:17

This verse is a powerful reminder of what makes relationships thrive—respect, love, reverence for God, and a willingness to honor the roles He's set in place. It encourages us to live in harmony with others and to reflect Christ's character in how we treat those around us.

In marriage, these principles are significant. Respect is the foundation of a strong relationship—when spouses treat each other with kindness and honor, they reflect God's love. Loving the family of believers reminds us that we're not meant to do life alone; the church community can offer support, encouragement, and prayer when we need it most. And fearing God means keeping Him at the center of our marriage, trusting His guidance above everything else.

Finally, honoring authority reminds us of the value of humility and submission—not in weakness, but as an act of obedience to God. When we live by these principles, our marriage becomes a testimony of God's grace and order to the world. How can you show more respect and honor to your spouse in daily interactions? This week, choose one way to show respect to your spouse through words or actions. For example, speak kindly during disagreements or express gratitude for their efforts.

Father, thank You for the gift of marriage and the opportunity to grow in love and respect. Help us to honor You in our relationship by showing kindness, humility, and reverence for one another. May our marriage reflect Your glory and be a light to others. Guide us in living out Your word this week. Amen.

Week 49: Honoring Each Other in Love

Father, we come before You with humble hearts, seeking to grow in love and honor within our marriage. Help us to live out Your word by putting each other first, showing devotion, and reflecting Your sacrificial love in our relationship. Teach us to be more like You in how we love and serve one another. Amen.

"Be devoted to one another in love. Honor one another above yourselves."

— Romans 12:10

God calls us to love selflessly, putting others before ourselves. This verse challenges us to build a love rooted in devotion, loyalty, and honor. In marriage, that means seeing your spouse as a partner—a gift from God—worthy of respect and care.

True devotion isn't just about showing up when things are easy; it's about staying committed through every high and low. Honoring your spouse means listening to their thoughts, appreciating their strengths, and making them feel valued. When we choose to love this way, we reflect Christ's deep, unconditional love—the foundation of a strong, godly marriage. How can you be more intentional in showing devotion to your spouse? This week, pick one small way to serve them—tackle a chore they don't enjoy, cook their favorite meal, or offer extra encouragement during a stressful time.

Lord, thank You for the gift of marriage and the opportunity to grow in love and devotion. Help us to honor one another as You honor us, serving selflessly and with joy. Strengthen our bond so that we reflect Your glory in our marriage. May our love for each other draw us closer to You and be a testimony of Your goodness to the world. In Jesus' name, Amen.

Week 50: Honoring Each Other's Gifts

Lord, we come before You with grateful hearts for the unique gifts You have given us. Thank you for how You have called us to serve, individually and as a couple. Help us to honor You by using these gifts for Your glory, strengthening our marriage, and building up those around us. Unite us in Your Spirit, Lord, to reflect Your love and purpose in all we do. Amen.

"There are different kinds of gifts, but the same Spirit distributes them. There are different kinds of service, but the same Lord. There are different kinds of working, but in all of them and in everyone it is the same God at work."

—1 Corinthians 12:4-6 (NIV)

This passage reminds us that God uniquely gifts every person, and those gifts are meant to work together in harmony under the guidance of the same Spirit. In the context of marriage, this is a powerful reminder that God has equipped each spouse with talents and strengths to complement one another. Marriage is not just a union of two people but a partnership designed by God to reflect His love and purpose.

Understanding and valuing each other's differences can transform challenges into opportunities for growth and deeper connection. As you each bring your gifts into the marriage, you create a union that glorifies God and serves others. Whether through acts of service, encouragement, leadership, or compassion, God is at work through your partnership.

What unique gifts do you see in your spouse, and how can you celebrate those gifts this week? Are there areas in your marriage where you can better collaborate, using your strengths for a shared purpose? Take time this week to express gratitude for the gifts you see in your spouse. Share specific examples of how their strengths have blessed your marriage or others.

Gracious God, thank You for the unique ways You have gifted us and brought us together in marriage. Please help us see and celebrate those gifts with one another. Teach us to serve in unity, reflecting Your love to the world around us. May we lean on Your Spirit to guide us, strengthen us, and use us for Your glory. We trust in Your work in our lives and our marriage. In Jesus' name, we pray. Amen.

Father, we come before You with humble hearts, seeking wisdom and discernment. Help us recognize the influences in our lives and protect our marriage from anything that draws us away from Your will. Let us surround ourselves with relationships that build us up in faith and strengthen our union as a reflection of Your love. In Jesus' name, we pray. Amen.

"Do not be deceived: 'Evil company corrupts good habits.'"

— 1 Corinthians 15:33 (NIV)

This verse warns us about the power of influence. It reinforces the saying to be careful who your friends are. The people we allow into our lives shape our behaviors, attitudes, and, ultimately, our character. In the context of marriage, this truth takes on even greater significance. If we surround ourselves with individuals or influences that disrespect God's design for marriage, it can weaken the bond between spouses. Gossip, negativity, or advice contradicting biblical principles can sow discord, but seeking godly companionship fosters love, respect, and encouragement.

Paul's words are a call to be vigilant about the company we keep. Within marriage, this means guarding your relationship against toxic influences and seeking community with those who uplift, encourage, and model Christ-like love. Are there any influences in your life that may negatively impact your marriage or spiritual walk? How can you intentionally invite Godly influences into your marriage this week? Take time this week to assess the relationships in your life as a couple. Identify any friendships or connections that may be drawing you away from God's principles and discuss how you can set boundaries.

Lord, thank You for the gift of marriage and the blessing of relationships that encourage and uplift us. Please help us to guard our hearts and our union by being mindful of the company we keep. Surround us with godly influences that strengthen our bond and draw us closer to You. We trust You to guide us in love, wisdom, and unity. In Jesus' name, Amen.

Heavenly Father, thank You for the gift of love and for showing us the perfect example through Your Son. Help us to clothe ourselves in love that brings unity and peace, not only in our individual lives but also in our marriage. Teach us to reflect Your love in our words, actions, and thoughts as we grow together in harmony. Amen.

"And above all these put on love, which binds everything together in perfect harmony."

— Colossians 3:14

This verse calls believers to intentionally "put on" love, as one would clothe themselves. Love is the ultimate virtue that completes and unifies all others, creating harmony and unity. In marriage, love is the glue that binds two individuals together despite their differences. Through love, forgiveness flows, understanding deepens, and peace abounds. Just as Christ's love holds the Church together, our love for one another holds our marriage in balance, ensuring that every decision, every word, and every action reflects His heart.

When love is at the center of a marriage, it creates an environment where both partners can thrive spiritually and emotionally. This verse reminds us that love isn't just a feeling but a deliberate choice we must make daily to foster harmony and unity. How does Christ's example of sacrificial love challenge how you approach disagreements or misunderstandings in your relationship? This week, choose one intentional act of love that prioritizes your spouse's needs above your own.

Lord, thank You for the reminder that love is the foundation of harmony. Help us actively clothe ourselves in love daily, seeking to honor You and one another. May Your love guide our actions, soften our hearts, and strengthen our bond as a couple. Teach us to serve each other humbly and gracefully so that our marriage reflects Your perfect unity. We commit our relationship into Your hands, trusting in Your guidance and provision. In Jesus' name, Amen.

Our marriages should be filled with peace and joy. They should mimic the love that Christ has for the Church. Let your marriage be an example of that unconditional love. No matter what challenges come your way, face them together, and remember the love you share for each other. I leave you with some basic principles that will make a drastic difference in any marriage by Jimmy Evans.

- The most critical issue in marriage is a personal relationship with Jesus Christ.

- Marriage must be the priority after God.

- Marriage is work. There is no such thing as a marriage that operates solely on chemistry.

- Marriage requires teamwork and sacrifice.

- Men and women are very different and must honor each other's unique natures and roles. Work hard to meet each other's needs.

- Marriage takes faith.

- Couples must deal with anger head-on and not go to bed with unresolved issues.

- One spouse trusting in God and doing the right thing can turn the worst marriage around.

Keeping the Covenant Strong

Now that you've walked through this journey of faith, love, and growth, you have everything you need to strengthen your marriage through God's design. But your journey doesn't stop here.

By sharing your honest thoughts about this book on Amazon, you can help other couples find the same encouragement and wisdom. **Scan the QR code below and your review could be why another husband and wife invite God deeper into their relationship.**

Thank you for being part of this mission. A godly marriage is a lifelong journey, and when we share what we've learned, we help others walk this path with faith and confidence.

With gratitude,

B. Mitchell-Dos Santos & Phelipe Dos Santos

References

Beyer, K. (2018, May 13). *Biblical headship & submission*. Marriage Enrichment. ACC Counseling. https://accounseling.org/marriage/maritalenrichment/biblical-headship-submission/

Christian Parenting. (n.d.). *Yes, you need a marriage mentor* (A. Startz, Author). https://www.christianparenting.org/articles/yes-you-need-a-marriage-mentor/

Deal, R. (2016, November 29). *The smart blended marriage*. Focus on the Family. https://www.focusonthefamily.com/marriage/the-smart-blended-marriage/

Evans, J. (2009, March 1). *One: A marriage devotional*. XO Publishing.

Family Life. (2016). *7 steps for starting a marriage ministry*. https://www.familylife.com/uncategorized/7-steps-for-starting-a-marriage-ministry/

Fletcher, T. (2024). *Marriage: Building a foundation of faith*. Family Today.

https://www.familytoday.com/relationships/marriage-building-a-foundation-of-faith/

Gaspard, T. (2024, February 6). *10 ways to rekindle the passion in your marriage.* The Gottman Institute. https://www.gottman.com/blog/10-ways-rekindle-passion-marriage/

Koster, D. (2021, November 7). *Biblical guidelines for sexually healthy relationships.* Family Fire. https://familyfire.com/articles/biblical-guidelines-for-sexually-healthy-relationships

National University. (n.d.). *The dangers of social media on marriage and family.* https://www.nu.edu/blog/the-dangers-of-social-media-on-marriage-and-family/

New International Version Bible. (2011). *The Holy Bible, New International Version.* Zondervan.

Paine, C., & Bentley, C. (2024, July 25). *Marriage and money: What does God expect?* Focus on the Family. https://www.focusonthefamily.com/marriage/marriage-and-money-what-does-god-expect/

Seattle Christian Counseling. (2015, January 26). *Effective conflict resolution techniques for couples.* https://seattlechristiancounseling.com/articles/5-helpful-bible-verses-about-conflict-resolution-in-your-marriage

Slattery, J. (2015, November 10). *Rekindling intimacy*. Focus on the Family. https://www.focusonthefamily.com/marriage/rekindling-intimacy/

Sypert, J. (2018, September 23). *A union that reveals a mystery* [Sermon]. Preston Highlands Church. https://prestonhighlands.org/2018/09/23/a-union-that-reveals-a-mystery/

Tacoma Christian Counseling. (2019, October 30). *God's plan for sexual intimacy: 4 principles for married couples*. https://tacomachristiancounseling.com/articles/gods-plan-for-sexual-intimacy-4-principles-for-married-couples

Valenzuela, S., Halpern, D., & Katz, J. E. (2014). Social network sites, marriage well-being, and divorce: Survey and state-level evidence from the United States. *Computers in Human Behavior, 36*, 94-101. https://www.sciencedirect.com/science/article/abs/pii/S0747563214001563

Cover Designer: SantoRoy
Cover Image: Shutterstock
Standard License
Asset ID: 1772593994